Apri[l] ████████

Dear ██████ ████

and ████████

with pleasure

I present you

with this

little volume.

████████ ██████████

May Peace Be With You

Other books by Richard L. Evans

◆

UNTO THE HILLS

THIS DAY . . . AND ALWAYS

. . . AND "THE SPOKEN WORD"

AT THIS SAME HOUR

TONIC FOR OUR TIMES

FROM THE CROSSROADS

THE EVERLASTING THINGS

FROM WITHIN THESE WALLS

MAY
PEACE
BE WITH YOU

by

RICHARD L. EVANS

HARPER & BROTHERS, PUBLISHERS
New York

To Alice—
and home
and family
and friends
Who give much meaning to
all the opportunities of time
and all the assurances of eternity

"And as the evening twilight fades away
The sky is filled with stars, invisible by
  day."
                              —Henry W. Longfellow

Contents

[7]

Youth—and the
Future

A Man—And
His Work

"Thou Art What Thou
Art"

Some Essential Qualities
of Character

Self-control, and Liberty,
and Law . . .

Happiness, Comparisons, and a
Quiet Conscience

[11]

Foreword

This book begins with an awareness of the importance of people and of living with them—in marriage, the home, school, business, and in all relationships of life—with a recognition of our need of others always.

It ends with some attitudes of age, with a look at what we do with life, and the hopeful endlessness of opportunity: "Where one door closes, another opens. . . ."

As we move with "Music and the Spoken Word" toward our second third of a century, we are soberingly aware that these more than threescore years have gone with exceeding swiftness. As this program has come to be the longest, continuously presented nation-wide broadcast, the passing years have made us more aware that we owe much to many:

To the Tabernacle Choir, its staff and officers and organists, whose music is known and loved and understood world-wide.

To KSL and CBS, and the men of radio everywhere, who help us reach world-wide.

To the listeners, who take time to listen, who take time to write, or who take time to come and bring with them their words of kindly encouragement.

To secretaries and associates, without whose help the meeting of the pressure of an ever-present deadline would at times hardly appear to be possible.

In brief acknowledgments in eight preceding books we have sometimes named names and sometimes have not. There is hazard in doing so, because always there are omissions. But letting past acknowledgments stand as they are, we feel we must now mention some among many whose help or confidence and encouragement are part of what makes possible this weekly preparation and performance: President David O. McKay; Geniel Robbins, Beverly Harrison, and Shirley Matthews; Marba Josephson; Paul H. Evans, Richard A. Welch, Ray E. Loveless, and J. Allen Jensen; Lester F. Hewlett, Richard P. Condie, Jay Welch, Alexander Schreiner, Frank W. Asper, Mary Jack, and J. Russell Scott.

This broadcast has been something of a search for a common denominator, and we are grateful for the conviction that in part at least we may have found one, as the language of uplifting music gives setting for some timeless and eternal truths:

—grateful for the faith that there are some fixed and glorious purposes and principles that can be counted on;

—grateful that the world, the universe, is ordered by a Wisdom and Intelligence infinitely beyond us all, the Father of us all, who made us in His image;

—and grateful that life with all its problems, disappointments, hopes, and opportunities is well worth all the searching and the seeking, all the doing and enduring, as time moves us on into the endlessness of eternity.

Such is the essence of the two- to three-minute topics which appear in these pages—and which are mingled with the music of the Tabernacle Choir and Organ—from the Crossroads of the West—from Temple Square in Salt Lake City—on CBS Radio each Sunday.

RICHARD L. EVANS

"To Live in Right Relations..."

"If it were possible to live in right relations with men! . . . Could we not deal with a few persons—with one person—after the unwritten statutes, and make an experiment of their efficacy?"[1]

—Emerson

Marriage—and Character

What we have in our hearts to say could be said at any time, at many times; for it pertains to the goodness and purpose of life and to the peace and happiness of all who marry—and of children—and to the whole future of families.

First of all, marriage must be coupled with character. It requires character to live in this closest of all relationships of life. Marriage requires also kindly consideration, the overlooking of many small things, and an earnest disposition not to find fault. Anyone could annoy anyone at times, and anyone who looks for faults and flaws will surely find them.

Marriage requires companionship and encouragement and confidence, and kindly, forthright frankness—not holding within the small resentments, the hurts of heart, and not sitting and brooding in silence. It requires keeping things out in the open, freely talking out problems as equal partners.

It requires also, solvency, with a realistic regard for income and outgo—with organized ambition and effort to get ahead, and with a measure of contentment as to what cannot *now* be reasonably reached.

Marriage requires self-control. There is no place in a good marriage for ill-tempered utterance or quick condemnation, or for selfishness or selfish indulgence. It requires loyalty and faithfulness and moral cleanliness.

No marriage should be allowed to become commonplace. Neglected or abused, it may possibly be brought back to what it once was, but it is better to keep it sweet and wholesome from the first so that there may be no scars.

But if offenses should come, let there be forgiving and let there be forgetting, always with the earnest intent of making this relationship last—for every privilege carries with it an obligation and every child brought into the world is a real responsibility, and marriage must be founded on firm foundations.

Marriage is the most complete commitment of life, and as such should receive the best effort of all who enter into it. It must include willing work, sincere service, respect for each other, respect of self, humility and prayerfulness, and the healing power of love, and faith and common convictions—faith in God, faith in the future, and faith in the everlasting things of life. And to you who venture into marriage—and to you who have and to you who ever will—remember that respect and love and confidence must be earned every day, with encouragement and faithfulness and sincere consideration.

...But Marriage Is Another Matter...

"Do you expect, forsooth," asked an ancient Roman writer, "that a mother will hand down to her children principles which differ from her own?"[2]

This compelling question could well be asked by all who contemplate marriage, and who are wise enough to look beyond the present to the time when there are children, and to all the hoped-for years of life and to the everlastingness of life.

It is possible for two people to enjoy the company of each other in many ways, with wide differences of preference and opinion, of habits, of teaching, of training, of background and belief. Indeed, a diversity of friendships is one of life's real enrichments. To learn of the goodness of those who are unlike—their worth, their sincerity, their good hearts, their good minds, their good company—is rich and rewarding. It is wonderful to have a wide range of choice friends who can be counted on, friends who can be enjoyed and loved and trusted. Such is the meaning of friendship.

But marriage is very much another matter. In the partnership of two parents a unity of purpose is vitally essential, for it involves the training, the teaching of children, the molding of character, the sense of values, the foundations, the interpretation, the very purpose of life, its ultimate and everlasting meaning. And in a matter so momentous, how could there be a clear course, unless objectives and convictions were compatible, or unless one or the other or both set their convictions aside—which would hardly be a safe or firm foundation for best understanding or for setting a sure and certain course.

"Observe how soon, and to what a degree, a mother's influence begins to operate!"[3] suggested one writer, to which another added: "The mother in her office holds the key of the soul; and she it is who stamps the coin of character."[4]

Life is largely a reflection of what people believe plus what they have the courage and conviction to stand for, to live for. And this observation anciently offered, has much in it for reflection for those who will make the momentous decision of marriage: Do you expect anyone—could you expect anyone—could you expect fathers or mothers —to hand down to their children principles which differ from their own?

The Chasms That Keep Us from Understanding

Shakespeare, in *Love's Labour's Lost*, had one of his characters make this remark: "Who understandeth thee not, loves thee not."[5] We so much need an understanding of each other, at home, at school, at work, in marriage, and in every relationship of life.

One of the barriers to understanding is lack of communication, lack of talking things out, lack of keeping things in the open. One of the barriers to happiness and trust and confidence in marriage is this very matter. Even the most promising marriage, the most promising relationship of life, can run into trouble if either party to the partnership will sit in brooding silence, will nurture and closely hug his grievances to his heart, and not be frank and honest and open.

Pressures build up when there isn't any outlet. Small things become magnified, and much more than is true may be imagined. And so homes and hearts are needlessly broken, and sacred covenants sometimes severed.

No two people ever see all things precisely the same. Often two people even closely associated fail to have the same sense of humor. What seems funny to one may seem pointless to another. What was meant as a harmless, good-humored remark by one person, may, to another, seem to have a sharp or sarcastic edge on it—or a meaning which honestly may not have been meant.

And so there is much of misunderstanding, much of not knowing, of not talking, of not getting through, of not seeing inside; much of hurt, much of heartache, much of mistrust, much of unhappiness, and sitting in hurt silence. Any two people, any number of people, who are not understanding, not congenial, not getting through to those with whom they should keep closer, should open up, communicate, take off the tenseness, the quickness to feel offended, and talk and face facts, not in self-justification, and not in accusation, but in frank and honest fairness without any edge on it—and not sit and brood in silence.

Happiness cannot survive in pent-up places. It flourishes out in the open. And among friends and families, neighbors and fellow workers, and among those married, we must talk; we must get through, we must somehow cross the chasms that keep us from understanding one another.

The Ignorance That Shuts
Out Understanding

"If one only wished to be happy, this could be easily accomplished; but we wish to be happier than other people, and this is always difficult, for we believe others to be happier than they are."[6]

One of the greatest barriers to happiness is ignorance. And this we say despite the old saying that ignorance is bliss. If it is, it is a bliss founded on false foundations. Happiness should be, must be—indeed, basically has to be—founded on fact, on truth and intelligence. Consider in a few sentences the ignorance that pertains to the problem of getting along with people, the ignorance that shuts out understanding, that creates mistrust, intolerance, and contention:

"The earth and the fullness thereof has been placed at the disposal of Man," wrote Hendrik Van Loon in his *Geography*. "This home of ours is a good home. It produces . . . benefits in . . . abundant measure. . . . But Nature has her own code of laws. . . . Nature will give unto us and she will give without stint, but in return she demands that we study her precepts and abide by her dictates. It will take time, it will take . . . slow and painful education to make us find the true road of salvation. But that road leads towards the consciousness that we are all of us fellow-passengers on one and the same planet. Once we have got hold of this absolute verity—once we have realized and grasped the fact that for better or for worse this is our common home . . . that it therefore behooves us to behave as we would if we found ourselves on board a train or a steamer bound for an unknown destination—we shall have taken the first but most important step towards the solution of that terrible problem which is at the root of all our difficulties. We are all of us fellow-passengers on the same planet . . . and we are all of us equally responsible for the happiness and well-being of the world in which we happen to live."

With this awareness we would plead with all people to penetrate the shadows, to dispel ignorance and invite understanding, because what affects any of us affects all of us. And all of us earnestly need understanding—understanding of ourselves, understanding of other people and their problems. Ignorance is an enemy. It is not happiness.

"This home of ours is a good home"[7]—but more and more we need to cross the chasms that keep us from understanding, from communicating as man to man, for we are, all of us, fellow-passengers on the same planet. We need to learn to get along.

On Getting Along with People

One of the most important things in life is learning to get along with the people we have to live with. The question of peace itself—at home and world-wide—revolves around our being able to do just this. Living literally alone is seldom possible and seldom desirable, but living in daily association with others means either fighting with them or learning to get along with them.

There are many apparent ways of getting along with people, some of which are acceptable and some of which are not. One of the most plausibly apparent, but also one of the most fallacious, is to eliminate all differences by force—to make everyone think and act alike. Another fallacious way is completely to give up our own views and try to do everything that everyone else wants us to do. Such extremes, of course, are untenable. They could not be accomplished in the first place, and even if they could, they offer no real solution to the problem of getting along with people.

Less extreme, but still fallacious, is the assumption that getting along with others necessarily means the compromise of our own standards and ideals and principles. Compromising standards isn't getting along with people. It is merely self-betrayal —retreat. It is appeasement, it is buying peace at any price; and appeasement where principles and standards and truth and moral right are concerned is but the beginning of more problems.

And so the question still remains: How to get along with people who don't think alike, who have different standards and different interests? It is practical and possible to do so, as is daily demonstrated by countless men and women who live in the same world, in the same town, and even in the same homes with others of different likes, different interests, different convictions, and who do get along together without compromising principles.

But the moment we do compromise any of our principles we stand in danger of being forced to compromise all of our principles; for the moment we step across the line of principle there is no other borderline at which to stop. After the first compromise all other compromises are merely a matter of degree.

And so, keeping peace among friends, and even among strangers, involves, whenever occasion calls for it, in making known what we stand for and why, in staying squarely with our ideals and convictions, and respecting and defending all others in a like privilege.

In short, the way to get along with people is to *know* what we ought to be, to *be* what we ought to be, to give respect and to demand respect, and not resort to bluffing, appeasement, or compromise on any point of principle.

The Person-to-Person Equation

In our increasingly organized way of life we tend to classify people and problems, to institutionalize all service, to set up many rules and regulations. And in this "departmentalization of problems," people have to qualify under what seem to be rigid requirements before they can benefit from particular plans and programs.

Because human judgment is so variable, and because human problems are so complex, organized effort has to come somewhat within definable categories, within certain procedures. All this, in a measure, is somewhat necessarily so.

But we should not let the organizing of services isolate us from a sense of personal responsibility when we find a personal need. Routine is all right in routine matters, and theory is all right when it works; but when a real person with a real problem presents himself, when the need is evident and obvious, and when we personally have been appealed to, we can scarcely quiet conscience by referring to a rule that says under such and such a section you cannot qualify.

Suppose a man is ill. Suppose a child is lost. Suppose someone is injured and needs help from the first person who appears. There are times when, in a personal way, we have to set aside the excluding and qualifying clauses and simply do something—even if it isn't routine, even if it isn't convenient, even if it *is* after hours.

In order to avoid personal appeals people are sometimes heard to say, "If I do this for you, I'll have to do it for everyone else"—giving this as the reason for not doing something for someone who needs it now! With all respect to precedents and procedures and not presuming to set any of them aside, yet there is this to be considered: If we couldn't do for anyone what we couldn't do for everyone, we couldn't ever do anything for anyone.

Institutions and organizations must necessarily regulate themselves and define their functions—but the Parable of the Good Samaritan would still seem to suggest the need for the person-to-person equation—would still seem to suggest that we should do what we can do for someone when the need is now, when the problem is presented.

If we couldn't do anything for anyone that we couldn't do for everyone, we could never do anything for anyone.

Thoughtfulness . . .

As the seasons pass, we long for a pausing from the fevered pace, from the rush and the routine, for the quieting of the spirit, for the slowing of the pulse, for an appraisal of life's purpose, and for thoughtfulness for people and their problems.

We sometimes wonder what others think of us, but most of the time they do not think of us at all. Often they are so absorbed with their own thoughts, with their own problems, with the impressions *they* are making on others, that they are all but unaware of us, even as we are often unaware of them—except perhaps somewhat superficially.

But with thoughtfulness we learn to know that every person has his problems, that no one can always be at his best, that every one has good days and bad, times of encouragement and times of downright despondency.

With thoughtfulness we learn that what seemed to be a slight may not have been intended so at all—and we learn not to be supersensitive, not to imagine offenses that are not intended. With thoughtfulness we learn to deal gently with the lives and the hurts and the hearts of others, and to hold the tongue and the temper. We learn to see the problems of those who are younger, who

need understanding and kindness and encouragement—and also of those who are older, who, for a
different reason, need understanding and kindness
and encouragement.

With thoughtfulness we learn to live with problems that seem all but insoluble. We learn to hold
on, to wait for a mood to change, for people to
modify, for the difficult day to pass. We learn
something of the enduring values. We learn patience and prayerfulness and understanding—faith
for the present hour, and faith for the future.

*   *   *

"More hearts pine away in secret an-
guish for unkindness from those who
should be their comforters, than for any
other calamity in life."[8]

—Edward Young

"Love at Home"

"The days grow shorter, the nights grow
longer, the headstones thicken along
the way; but love grows stronger
for those who walk with us day by day."[9]
—Ella Wheeler Wilcox

"Love at Home..."

An able physician recently suggested three short questions that could be asked to indicate how well a particular person might adjust to troubles and tensions: If the patient or the person can answer "yes" to these three questions, he is probably not seriously neurotic, this professional source said:

"1) Did your parents love each other? 2) Did they love their children? 3) Did the children love their parents?"[10]

If the answer to these three short questions is a solid and sincere "yes," it is likely that many if not most of life's emotional problems can solidly be met and solved.

This we offer as evidence of some things most to be thankful for. Among the blessings of life for which there is reason for surpassing gratitude are the company and confidence, the love and loyalty of family. Whatever else a man may have, if these he doesn't have, life is a duration of less than much it might have been.

With an understanding family, life is made up of many things: the closeness of companionship, the give and take, the sharing with and caring for.

There is the discipline; the acting as we are; the saying what we mean—and sometimes seeming to say what we don't mean; sometimes taking much for granted, sometimes seeming indifferent—which isn't actually indifference, and quickly turns to deep concern in time of need, in time of trouble. There is the going, the returning, the diversity of interests; the sense of belonging; the unforgettable feelings of affection; the unforgettable mixture of memories that hold tight our hearts, and strongly pull us back wherever we are—all this is home, all this is family, all this and more than ever can be mentioned:

Love at home. The love of parents. The love of children. The love of loved ones for one another. These are among the greatest of the gifts that God has given—these things more precious than ever we could be adequately thankful for—these things recalled in an old and cherished hymn:

> "There is beauty all around
> When there's love at home.
> There is joy in every sound
> When there's love at home.
>
> Peace and plenty here abide,
> Smiling sweet on every side.
> Time doth softly, sweetly glide
> When there's love at home . . . ."[11]

Mothers—and Their Love and Loyalty

What constantly is close to us is likely to become commonplace and it often takes perspective to know how much it means. This would be true of mothers, in our awareness of how much *they* mean.

If we are most fortunate, we are so close to them in our years of youth, that we hardly have occasion to appraise the part they perform. So well they keep things running that we are hardly aware of what they do to keep things running well. So well they take off the edge of our deeper disappointments that we hardly realize how well they comfort and encourage.

We may sometimes be impatient; we may sometimes seem annoyed by their teaching and restraint, by their counsel and concern. But in our less emotional, more reasonable moments, even early in life we seem somewhat to sense their strength, their service, and their selflessness, and some meaning of their love and loyalty. And even early, we somewhat sense the emptiness we feel in their absence, with some intuitive awareness of how much they one day will be missed.

Many have sought to say what mothers have meant. "My mother was an angel upon earth . . . ,"

said John Quincy Adams, "Her heart was the
abode of heavenly purity. She had no feelings but
of kindness and beneficence. . . . She had known
sorrow, but her sorrow was silent. . . . If there is
existence and retribution beyond the grave, my
mother is happy."[12]

From her childhood, Louisa May Alcott recalled
these lines of kindly encouragement from a note
left in her room by her mother: "I have observed
all day your patience with baby, your obedience
and kindness to all. Go on trying, my child. God
will give you strength and courage. I shall say a
little prayer over you in your sleep. Mother."[13]

Such kindly memories of mother inspired the
poet to write these later lines:

Faith that withstood the shocks of toil and time;
  Hope that defied despair;
  Patience that conquered care;
And loyalty, whose courage was sublime;
The great deep heart that was a home for all,—
  Just, elequent, and strong
  In protest against wrong;
Wide charity, that knew no sin, no fall;
The Spartan spirit that made life so grand,
  Mating poor daily needs
  With high, heroic deeds,
That wrested happiness from Fate's hard hands.[14]

It is a hallowed thing to have such memories
of mothers. May mothers, in the sacred trust of
righteous motherhood, continue to make such
memories; and may we always remember mothers
and the blessed memories they make.

"Whatever Else She Is . . ."

In considering ideals and objectives, and the sometimes overemphasis on social considerations, and appeals merely to appearance, Ruskin wrote: "The courage or sincerity [of girls is hardly] thought of half so much importance as their way of coming in at a door; . . . [We bring] for the purpose of our own pride, the full glow of the world's worst vanity upon a girl's eyes, at the very period when the whole happiness of her future . . . depends upon her remaining undazzled . . ."

Thus he appeals for simple standards, solid values, for the lasting things—indeed the everlasting things—of life, not unduly emphasizing the sometimes shallow externals or the sometimes superficial social show.

As to competition between the sexes he said, "We are foolish, and without excuse foolish, in speaking of the 'superiority' of one sex to the other, as if they could be compared . . . Each completes the other, and is completed by the other. . . . You may chisel a boy into shape, as you would a rock, or hammer him into it, if he be of a better kind, as you would a piece of bronze. But you cannot hammer a girl into anything. She grows as a flower does . . . you cannot fetter her; she must take her own fair form and way, and have—'Her household motions light and free, And steps of virgin liberty.' "[15]

[37]

With the citing of these words we would summarize again by saying that despite woman's so-called emancipated place, and her many added opportunities, there are some things she should continue to be, whatever else she is: the mother, the wife, the helpmate and homemaker, the true and virtuous teacher of children, the symbol of service, of purity and compassion, and of the living of a good and gracious life—not the competitor of men, the pawn of men, the partaker of men's vices, the reflection of men, but something which she should be for herself, except for which there would be a letting down rather than a lifting of our lives.

Fathers Are to Talk to . . .

There are some wonderful words in our language, words that are inseparably associated: home, mother, father, family—and in our thoughts they are linked in fondest and most meaningful remembrance.

Where the normal pattern prevails, father is more away and less closely acquainted with the daily problems and program. But fathers are people in whose footsteps sons are apt to follow, and with whose hearts daughters are likely to have their way.

Fathers are people by whose name the family is known. Fathers are people whom sons and daughters should feel free to approach with their problems. There are hazards in going it alone in life, and fathers are to talk to—even if they seem to be too busy; even if they are doing so much for the family in other ways that they are not enough at home.

Some three centuries ago John Locke said, ". . . a father will do well, as his son grows up, . . . to talk familiarly with him; . . . The sooner you treat him as a man, the sooner he will begin to be one: and if you admit him into serious discourses . . . with you, you will . . . raise his mind above the usual amusements of youth, and those trifling occupations which it is commonly wasted in. . . .

[39]

And I cannot but often wonder to see fathers who love their sons very well, yet so order the matter . . . as if they were never to enjoy, or have any comfort from those they love best in the world. . . . Nothing cements and establishes friendship and good-will so much as confident communication . . . . Other kindnesses, without this, leave still some doubts, but when your son sees you open your mind to him, [he will know he has] a friend and . . . father. . . ."[16]

It is sobering when a father sees in his son himself, his mannerisms, his ways, his words. It is a great moment in life when a father sees a son grow taller than he, or reach farther. It is a blessed thing for fathers to see their sons exceed them.

God bless fathers—and bless the sons and daughters who give fathers their greatest gift in the love they bear them, and in the virtuous, honorable, useful living of life.

"He That Will Have His
Son Respect Him . . ."

On the teaching and training of children, John Locke said: "For you must take this for a certain truth, that let them have what instructions you will, and ever so learned lectures . . . daily inculcated into them, that which will most influence their carriage will be the company they converse with, and the fashion of those about them."[16]

This impresses the importance of what we do, what we are, as compared with what we say— the words we speak, as compared with what others see in us and feel from us. And as to parents, as to teachers, as to all of us, never should we suppose that others will do what we say more surely than what they see us do.

"Manners, . . ." continued John Locke, "about which children are so often perplex'd and have so many goodly exhortations made them . . . are rather to be learnt by example than rules; . . . Having under consideration how great the influence of company is, and how prone we are all, especially children, to imitation, I must here take the liberty to mind parents of this one thing, viz., that he that will have his son have a respect for him and his orders, must himself have a great

[41]

reverence for his son. You must do nothing before him, which you would not have him imitate. . . . He will be sure to shelter himself under your example, . . . If you punish him for what he sees you practice yourself, he will . . . be apt to interpret it [as] the peevishness and arbitrary imperiousness of a father, who, without any ground for it, would deny his son the liberty and pleasures he takes himself. . . . Children (nay, and men too) do most by example. We are all a sort of [chameleons], that still take a tincture from things near us; nor is it to be wonder'd at in children, who better understand what they see than what they hear. . . ."[16]

These are sobering thoughts because of the responsibility they place upon us all. Beyond the mere routine of teaching, beyond the mere saying of sentences, beyond the mere speaking of repetitious truths—beyond all this, to be most effective and most convincing, we have to be, and should be, the living witnesses of the truth of what we teach.

* * *

"We never know the love of the parent till we become parents ourselves."[17]
—Henry Ward Beecher

The Teaching of a Child

"Be ever gentle with the children God has given you. Watch over them constantly; reprove them earnestly, but not in anger . . ."[18]

—Elihu Burritt

"Those First Speechless Years . . ."

It was written of John Ruskin that "the home atmosphere in which [he] grew up was one of utter peace and complete order. The relation between his father and mother was a beautiful one. There were no quarrels, no mysterious undercurrents of trouble or unhappiness so depressing to a sensitive child; and . . . the domestic machinery ran in well-ordered grooves."[19]

With this background it is understandable that Ruskin could later write these lines: "The education of a child begins in infancy. At six months old it can answer smile by smile, and impatience with impatience. It can observe, enjoy, and suffer. Do you suppose it makes no difference to it that the order of the house is perfect and quiet, the faces of its father and mother full of peace, their soft voices familiar to its ear, and even those of strangers, loving; or that it is tossed from arm to arm, [in a] . . . reckless . . . household, or [in] the confusion of a gay one? The moral disposition is, I doubt not, greatly determined in those first speechless years."[20]

"Children," said another observer, "are travellers newly arrived in a strange country of which they know nothing."[16] And yet another source said:

"Infancy isn't what it is cracked up to be. Children, not knowing that they are having an easy time, have a good many hard times. Growing and learning and obeying rules of their elders, or fighting against them, are not easy things to do."[21]

There is nothing more precious than a family, nothing more important than seeing a family established in righteous ways—and no wise parent would leave a child without early care and counsel and the example of the living of a righteous life.

The idea that we can leave entirely to children the choices of the vital essentials is unsafe. Leaving such decisions to the trial and error method is unsafe.

Children are entitled to counsel, and to knowing the principles that have been proved by the experience of the past. It is part of the heritage they have. They are entitled to example, to prayerful guidance, and righteous persuasion in the living of their lives. And even though they may react contrarily at times, they will be everlastingly grateful for early teachings taught, for early lessons learned, for the love and living example of a good parent's life.

"... Gentleness with Firmness ..."

"A young man before he leaves the shelter of his father's house," said John Locke, "should be fortified with resolution, . . . to secure his virtues, lest he should be led into some ruinous course, or fatal precipice, before he is sufficiently acquainted with the dangers . . ."[16]

Benjamin Franklin said, "Let thy child's first lesson be obedience, . . ."[22]

The idea that discipline and training should center outside the home is an altogether untenable idea. Contrary to what is sometimes supposed, studies on the subject suggest that youth would like to look to parents for the leadership, the guidance, without which they feel too foot-loose and unsure of themselves.

Reasonably, there comes the question: What are parents for? Not simply for food and shelter and physical necessities, although this is a great service in itself. But parents are also counselors, builders of character, teachers of truth, and must not abdicate their particular position as parents. They are those to whom God has given children, with the prime responsibility as the molders and shapers of manners and morals.

"With children," said Charles Haddon Spurgeon,

"we must mix gentleness with firmness.—They must not always have their own way, but they must not always be thwarted.—If we never have headaches through rebuking them, [when they are young] we shall have plenty of heartaches when they grow up."[23]

"An infallible way to make your child miserable," said Henry Home, "is to satisfy all his demands.—Passion swells by gratification; and the impossibility of satisfying every one of his wishes will oblige you to stop short at last after he has become headstrong."[24]

"Good Christian people," wrote Thomas Carlyle, "here [in your children] lies for you an inestimable loan;—take all heed thereof, in all carefulness employ it. With high recompense, or else with heavy penalty, will it one day be required back."[25]

The duty upon parents is much more than merely to provide. It is also to teach and train, to counsel, and, as necessary, correct—to *live* the part of parents, with gentleness and firmness so intermixed as never to avoid wise discipline or the doing of duty; to show forth leadership, and remember never to leave out love.

Who Teaches Early . . .

"Every man must sometime or other be trusted to himself."[16]

Pursuing further this thought and theme, we would share some observations as to fathers and sons, as to parents and children, and the urgent need for the earliest possible teaching and training:

"Would you have your son obedient to you when past a child"; asked John Locke, "be sure then to . . . imprint it in his infancy; . . . so shall you have him . . . obedient . . . whilst he is a child, and your affectionate friend when he is a man. . . . For the time must come, when [he] will be past the rod and correction; . . . and he that is a good, a virtuous, and able man, must be made so within. And therefore what he is to receive from education, what is to sway and influence his life, must be something put into him betimes; habits woven into the very principles of his nature, . . . The little, or almost insensible impressions on our tender infancies, have very important and lasting consequences."[16]

There is an old Greek proverb, often quoted, which says in substance: "He gives twice who gives quickly." It could be paraphrased to say, "He teaches twice who teaches early"—not when it is convenient only, not at some too long delayed a time, but when children are young, when they are with us—and not by what we tell them only, but by the living impressions we leave upon their lives —impressions they cannot and will not forget whether they are with us or away.

From John Locke we cite this sentence: "For you must take this for a certain truth, that let them have what instructions you will, and ever so learned lectures . . . daily inculcated into them, that which will most influence their carriage will be the company they converse with, and the fashion of those about them."[16]

Children . . . and the Effect of What They Feel . . .

"What gift," asked Cicero, "has Providence bestowed on man that is so dear to him as his children?"[26]

The answer suggests itself, and, since it is so, one thing of which we must be ever-mindful is the influence of attitudes and actions. We may say the right words; we may teach by rote; we may write the right lines, but the lives of youth are influenced by the full effect of all they feel and see and sense—by the tensions and standards and morals of the home, of family, and friends, of teachers, of the times. And no matter what we tell them, what they feel from us and see in us may be much more far-reaching than the routine of our teaching.

". . . For you must take this for a certain truth, that let them have what instructions you will, . . . that which will most influence their carriage will be the company they converse with, and the fashion of those about them. Children (nay, and men too) do most by example. . . ."[16]

We would add these further lines from John Locke: "Virtue is harder to be got than a knowledge of the world; and if lost in a young man, is seldom recover'd. . . . A young man before he

[51]

leaves the shelter of his father's house, . . . should be fortify'd with resolution, . . . to secure his virtues, lest he should be led into some ruinous course, or fatal precipice, before he is sufficiently acquainted with the dangers . . . and has steadiness enough not to yield to every temptation. . . . He that lays the foundation of his son's fortune in virtue and good breeding, takes the only sure and warrantable way. . . ."[16]

This, in the language of some three centuries ago, simply says that our children will be in large measure a reflection of the background of family and friends and of the moral environment in which they live their lives. "What gift has Providence bestowed on man that is so dear to him as his children?" This places upon parents the responsibility of setting such patterns as children may in safety pursue.

Letting Habits Harden

Time passes with exceeding swiftness between the time when we are very young and free and flexible until the time when thoughts and habits and attitudes become somewhat firmly fixed. And since fixed impressions, fixed standards, and the hardening of habits are so early in evidence, the beginnings of traits and tendencies are exceedingly significant:

Here are some sentences from John Locke on this important subject: "Parents," he said "being wisely ordain'd by nature to love their children, are very apt, . . . to cherish their faults too. They must not be cross'd, forsooth; they must be permitted to have their wills in all things; and they being in their infancies not capable of great vices, their parents think they may safely enough indulge their irregularities, and make themselves sport with that pretty perverseness which they think well enough becomes that innocent age. But to a fond parent, that would not have his child corrected for a perverse trick, but excus'd it, saying it was a small matter, Solon very well replied, 'Aye, but custom [the habit, the tendency] is no small matter.' . . . For you must always remember, that children [become] . . . men earlier than is thought. . . ."[16]

The beginnings are always exceedingly important.

[53]

William James thus summarized the subject: "Nothing we ever do is in strict scientific literalness wiped out. . . . Could the young but realize how soon they will become mere walking bundles of habits, they would give more heed to their conduct while in the plastic state. We are spinning our own fates, good or evil. . . . Every smallest stroke of virtue or of vice leaves its never so little scar. . . . We are . . . imitators and copiers of our past selves."[27]

It is true that an isolated act or instance may seem a small matter at the moment, but it is no small matter at any age to let a false standard get started, or to let a wrong habit harden.

Uprooting Too Many Times . . .

If we would fortify ourselves for the future as well as for meeting matters of the moment, we must learn to deal with young people so as not to keep them constantly in a state of ever-shifting uncertainty. If the prospects were to change from day to day, the scenes shift too frequently, if uncertainty should become chronic and capricious, it could conceivably produce a footloose generation—a generation lacking the confidence and incentive to prepare for the future.

There is a limit to the number of times that a tender plant can be disturbed without losing strength and growth and stability. When a plant or a person has been uprooted too many times, it isn't easy to take firm root again. And if we are not far-seeing in this particular problem, there is always present the possibility of destroying the seed of one of our greatest resources—the seed that would produce a perpetual harvest of competent, solid, resourceful, prepared people. The past has proved that cutting down forests without replanting impoverishes the future.

We may not match others in man power, but we may more than match them in skill and competence and technical training, and in resourcefulness in meeting emergencies—and we must see that it is so, not only now, but a decade from now, a generation from now.

We are not living in a settled time, but even in an unsettled time, there must be serious consideration for the future as well as for meeting matters of the moment. And youth must be encouraged to continue with calm purpose, not to be frustrated by the shifting uncertainties. We must conserve and save our material, mental, moral, and spiritual resources, and keep strong and prepared for the future by helping each generation to grow up with its roots down deep.

*   *   *

"God sends children . . . to enlarge our hearts; and to make us unselfish and full of kindly sympathies and affections; . . . My soul blesses the great Father, every day, that he has gladdened the earth with little children."[28]

—Mary Howitt

Youth—and the Future

"... Above all things the interest of your whole life depends on your being diligent, now, while it is called to-day . . ."[29]

—Carlyle

Youth—and Uncertainties and Decisions

Decisions are difficult for everyone—and perhaps especially for those who are pursuing or finishing their period of preparation: where to work, when to marry, how long to prepare, what commitments to make—decisions that affect the whole length of life, and that must be made despite the difficulties of settling down in unsettled situations.

As to all of these uncertainties and decisions, we would quote a short and sound sentence: "Fortune favors the best prepared people."[11]

There have always been uncertainities and there have always been decisions, and despite tensions and troubles and uncertain situations, there have never been more opportunities; there has never been more need for well-prepared people, or, that we are aware of, more appreciation or compensation for well-prepared people. And the passing uncertainties should not lead to short-sighted decisions or to cutting short the fullest possible preparation for fullest usefulness for the future.

Of course, the long broad look at life requires faith—and willingness to study, to work, and to wait—faith in the future.

And why not have faith in the future? Suppose

a generation of ten or twenty or thirty years ago had failed to have faith, suppose that their uncertainties had dissuaded them from preparing? Where would we turn today for prepared people? And what would *now* be their regrets for not preparing?

The late Charles F. Kettering said: "I object to people running down the future. I'm going to live all the rest of my life there."[30]

The future, young man, young woman, is where you are going to live the rest of your life. Have faith. Accept the uncertainties; don't brood about them. Avoid impatience, procrastination, enslaving habits, and time-wasting. Avoid debt as far as possible. Seek counsel. Have courage. Build solid foundations. Live with cleanliness and honor and high qualities of character. Accept the opportunities and obligations as they come. Be willing to work, to wait, to take responsibility.

Despite all uncertainties and unforeseen situations, the future will be better for the better prepared people. The future will be better for those who have the faith to finish, the faith to follow through.

Conscience and Habits
Away from Home

"There is nothing that a man can less afford to leave at home than his conscience or his good habits."[31] While this applies to all travel, to all activity, to all social situations, more particularly we have in mind the young who leave home for school, work, military service, or other purposes or pursuits. And we have in mind re-emphasizing that people are more important than place; that what a person is, is more important than where he is; that character and conduct are of utmost consequence always, everywhere.

If a person conducts himself well merely because of appearances, if his manners and morals are something to be shed when he is alone, or when he is away from family or friends, then he isn't really very safe or sound inside himself.

If those who go away should assume it to be a time for throwing off restraint, for letting loose, for careless conduct, for foolish and unworthy ways, they would pretty well have proved that they were immature, that they had not yet reached the time to be trusted to themselves.

There are several sides to consider when we are away from where we usually live our lives: one, that conduct cannot become coarse without

[61]

character becoming coarse; two, that always we live with conscience; that always we and the Lord God know what we are, whether others know it or not; that the record we make is our record no matter where we make it; three, that we can never be sure we are unseen, we can never count on not being known; and four, that always we have to live with ourselves.

And as to those who leave home for any purpose, there should be earnest remembrance of the faith and confidence and love of loved ones—of home, family, and friends, and of what is right for its own sake, aside from outside considerations. The lengthening of distance should not invite looseness, should not allow conduct to become careless. A person is what he is wherever he is, and "there is nothing [he] can less afford to leave [behind] than his conscience or his good habits."

"Every Man ... Must Be Trusted to Himself"

Concerning mental and physical and spiritual discipline, we cite some sentences from John Locke: "Consent to nothing but what may be suitable to the dignity and excellency of a rational creature. . . . The great principle and foundation of all virtue and worth is . . . this: that a man is able to deny himself his own desires, cross his own inclinations, . . . tho' the appetite lean the other way. . . ."[16]

And now briefly we should like to let John Locke introduce another subject for us with this short and significant sentence: "Every man must some time or other be trusted to himself; . . ."[16]

No matter how sheltered we may have been, or how much we may have depended on others, there do come times when we have to make our own choices, when we have to face facts, stand up to temptation, preserve principles; when we have to decide the course and accept the consequences. "Every man must some time or other be trusted to himself. . . ."

With the swiftly moving seasons, the time comes soon, or so it seems, when young people move out and away—from home, from family, from friends: some for further education, some for work, some for marriage, or other purposes. And at these times of taking leave from the long-felt influence of family and friends, parents and others also understandably feel some cause for concern. And well would they, except as sound principles have been instilled into the lives of those who leave.

And as for youth, well would they know that there do inevitably come times for choosing, for discriminating, for deciding for ourselves. Others cannot always go with us; others cannot always be watching; others cannot always make our choices, our decisions, or live our lives. There are countless times, when, by the necessity of circumstances, we have to decide for ourselves.

And to youth we would say: live by the sound and safe principles implanted in your hearts by righteous parents and teachers. And to parents and teachers we would say: implant sound principles as early as possible, by precept and by the righteous living of life. "Every man must some time or other be trusted to himself. . . ."[16] Blessed are they who early have implanted in their souls the foundations for facing these facts.

"Sound in Body, Mind, and Morals"

As to the balance we need for fullest effectiveness, we would recall some sentences on physical and mental and moral fitness, on wholeness in the living of life. It is, of course, possible to work, to serve, to accomplish many things without being well balanced, without peace and health and happiness, without the full and well-rounded living of life. Even a man with an unquiet conscience can account for some accomplishment. But how much more accomplishment could he account for if he had the poise that comes with peace, with an awareness of sound mental and moral and physical foundations.

One of the barriers to fitness is imbalance, excesses, the failure of what is sometimes called common sense. In the really healthy and happy man, there is a kind of wholeness—wholesomeness, we sometimes call it. "Wholesome" is a meaningful word which the dictionary defines as "spiritual or mental health or well-being . . . beneficial to character . . . sound in body, mind, and morals." It is the opposite of dissipation, of extremes and excesses; the opposite of immorality, of a brooding spirit, a clouded mind, a cluttered conscience; the opposite of harmful habits.

[65]

Wholesome is an awareness that "wickedness never was happiness,"[32] nor was anything else that upsets the harmonious working of mind and spirit and physical functioning. The sounder we are physically, mentally, morally, the safer we are, and the more effective and happier we are in the pursuit of life's great and wonderful purposes.

To cite again some lines from John Locke: "A sound mind in a sound body is a short, but full description of a happy state in this world. . . . The great principle and foundation of all virtue and worth is plac'd in this: that a man is able to deny himself his own desires, cross his own inclinations, . . . though the appetite lean the other way. . . ."[16] With wholesomeness come wisdom and knowledge and the peace of a quiet conscience.

Humility, Hard Work, and Integrity . . .

We are mindful these days of young people who are moving into life's more permanent pursuits. We are mindful also of the many decisions facing those who have completed some part of their preparation, and who must now or soon decide whether to quit or how far to proceed with further preparation.

It is difficult to generalize, for each case carries its own set of circumstances. But as to quitting, as to weariness of study, weariness of work, as to quitting because of discouragement, because of some uncertainy, or for some shortsighted considertion, this we would say, and say it most sincerely: Whatever we face in the future, the best-prepared people will be the best prepared for any eventuality. And whatever point young people may have reached they should go forth with faith and make solid plans, and prepare fully to live their lives.

We recall the recently reported counsel of an eminent American who suggested three factors for the solid living of life: The first is "humility." There is so much that all of us do not know. There is so much others have done for us. There is so much that to all of us the Lord God has given. Humility is a great and simple and essential quality of character.

[67]

The second is "hard work"—the willingness to work. We sometimes see the results; we see the flower, the fruit. We see what seems to be an overnight success. What we less often see are the roots down deep; the long working, the long waiting, the long period of preparation. No cause was ever served significantly without the earnest effort of preparing, improving, performing.

The third is "integrity."[33] There isn't anything that anyone has that is worth much without it. Talent isn't worth much without integrity; indeed, it is more likely a liability. No material possessions can be safeguarded or assured without integrity— and without it little business between people is possible. Integrity is the very essence of all satisfactory relationships in life.

To these three we would add a fourth—although not from the same source: courage, the courage to plan, to prepare, to work, to wait, to face facts: courage and faith in the future. Surely there are uncertainties. We none of us know how far our ventures will prosper, how long, how much we can profit by our preparation—but there is no promise to those who fail to prepare, to lay solid foundations, with humility, hard work, integrity, and courage—courage and faith for the future.

Belief, Faith, Courage . . .

There is a sentence accredited to William James, which says, "Our belief at the beginning of a doubtful undertaking is the one thing that insures the successful outcome of our venture."[34] This suggests comment on the question of belief, of faith, of courage: the will to succeed, the will to study, the will to know, the will to accomplish—even the will to live, which may at times be the difference between life and death.

The skeptics and the unbelievers play their parts, and they cannot be said to be unimportant parts, but progress principally is made by those who do things because they believe they can be done or don't know they can't be done—and yesterday's seemingly impossible performance has often become today's commonplace performance.

People often exceed their own past performance —or exceed other peoples' past performance. Contestants have often won when all the odds were to the contrary. Ventures have succeeded which seemed to hold little promise of success. Patients have recovered where it hasn't appeared to be possible. Men have survived when surely it seemed they couldn't. And often in these equations the intangible enters in: the spirit, the faith, the prayer, the will, the courage, the honest, earnest, believing, extra effort; the help, the strength that inexplicably comes from sources both within and outside ourselves.

If the pessimist had always been right, the world would have never have had any peace or progress. If the pessimist had always been right the world would have starved long since; nothing much would ever have been invented; nothing much would ever have been discovered; nothing much would ever have been improved.

Facts are surely not to be ignored, but are to be sought for and respected and taken into account in calculating all consequences. But besides the known facts there are always, or often, unknown facts. "There are more things in heaven and earth"[35] than we are aware of. And to those who have problems, to those who have sorrow or sickness, to those who have cherished dreams, high goals and ideals, and admirable objectives: Hold to hope, to courage; hold to faith; don't too soon succumb to hopelessness; keep faith in the future.

"Our belief at the beginning of a doubtful undertaking is the one thing that insures the successful outcome of our venture."

It All Adds Up . . .

We have become increasingly aware lately of the so-called exact sciences—of mathematical formulas, for example, from which can be forecast the forces of the inner atom and the orbiting of outer areas.

Order is evident in all of this—order, and the mind of an Infinite Administrator. But He, whose infinite orderliness is everywhere in evidence, has not left His children without laws of life that lead to results as sure, as certain, as the laws pertaining to physical phenomena—laws of health, moral laws, counsel, and commandments.

There has been a tendency by some to say that this age-old counsel on conduct may have served a purpose in the past, but is no longer essential to human happiness. But it simply is not so. There is no evidence that loose thinking or lax living or so-called emancipation from morals and manners has brought peace or happiness or progress to anyone—ever. And the Father of us all, in His love and wisdom pertaining to His children, hasn't said "Thou shalt" and "Thou shalt not" for no particular purpose.

As Emerson said: "The world looks like a multiplication-table or a mathematical equation, which, turn it how you will, balances itself. . . . You cannot do wrong without suffering wrong. . . . A man cannot speak but he judges himself. . . . Every secret is told, every wrong redressed, in silence and certainty. . . . The thief steals from himself. The swindler swindles himself. . . . Men suffer all their life long, under the foolish superstition that they can be cheated. But it is . . . impossible for a man to be cheated by anyone but himself. . . . What will you have? quoth God; pay for it and take it . . . thou shalt be paid exactly for what thou hast done, no more, no less."[36] To use the mathematical vernacular: It all adds up.

As William James worded it: "Every smallest stroke of virtue or of vice leaves its never so little scar."[27] Every thought and act and utterance is being counted "among the molecules and nerve cells and fibres." "Nothing we ever do is in strict scientific literaliness wiped out."[27]

No amount of rationalizing can cancel out the fact that peace and quiet come with keeping clean, with keeping the commandments, and no amount of rationalizing can save us from the consequences of misconduct. We are the sum of the thoughts we think, of the habits we have, of all we do and have done. We are the sum of all our actions and attitudes and utterances, of all things stored in body and mind and memory.

The laws given by a loving Father are always in force and always effective. His advice is worth taking, His commandments worth keeping. It all adds up.

* * *

"Unless a tree has borne blossoms in spring, you will vainly look for fruit on it in autumn."[37]

—August W. Hare

A Man—
and His Work

"Nothing is really work unless you would rather be doing something else."[38]
—Sir James M. Barrie

Work: Satisfaction and Shock Absorber

In living with ourselves, and in learning to live with life, work itself is one of life's surest satisfactions, and one of its surest shock absorbers. Work is much less wearing, much less wearisome than worry, and often it isn't so much the work men do that wears them away as the friction against which they do it—friction, and the frustration of not using life in a way that gives an inner peace and a deep-seated satisfaction.

Work is a basic law of life. The Lord God has so said. And the use of intelligence and talents and the creative and productive powers of mind and of muscle is expected of us. Without the dignity of work, without a sense of usefulness and accomplishment, men will surely deteriorate, will surely lose some self-respect, and the feeling of being a contributing part.

After all we owe a kind of rent, if we may call it that—or at least an obligation—for the space we occupy on earth, for the tenancy and tenure we have here, for the beauty and the sustenance, and the privilege of living life.

By reason of being alive we have a responsibility to study, learn, work, develop, contribute, serve, improve, to pay a debt to the past, to pay our way in the present, and to pass on something to the future. And there is waste—waste of time, of talent, of energy and effort, of life—and a quality of discontent without willing, useful work. The Lord God himself has set the example in his own creative activity, and there is every evidence in nature and the universe of an ever and on-going creative, productive process.

There is a building, strengthening, healing power in useful, willing work—work that doesn't unwillingly hold back. "Work," said Thomas Carlyle, "is the grand cure for all the maladies and miseries that ever beset mankind—honest work, which you intend getting done."[29] "Blessed is he who has found his work; . . ."[39] for work itself is one of life's surest satisfactions, and one of its surest shock absorbers.

"The Will to Work . . .
and Enjoy It"

These words of dedication from a grateful author currently appear in print: "To my own mother and father and to all parents like them, who have dedicated their lives to providing their children with the world's best inheritance—*The Will to work and the Wisdom to Enjoy It.*"[40] And then he adds this observation: "You just can't be miserable as long as you are properly and enjoyably busy; there is no room for misery. . . ."

This thought is further fortified with these words that come from some significant sources: "To have no regular work, no set sphere of activity,—what a miserable thing it is! . . . To have all . . . wants satisfied is something intolerable—the feeling of stagnation, which comes from pleasures that last too long."[41] "One must have leisure to be a pessimist; an active life almost always brings good spirits in body and in mind."[42] To this we would add the voice of Voltaire: "Not to be occupied, and not to exist, amount to the same thing. . . . One must give one's self all the occupation one can to make life supportable in this world. . . . The further I advance in age, the more I find work necessary. It becomes in the long run the greatest of pleasures, and takes the place of the illusions of life."[43]

One more witness we would add from a more recent source: "Inactivity, were it only for physiological reasons, is a torment to a healthy human being. . . . inactivity speedily becomes a torment as soon as the normal craving for rest and leisure has been satisfied. . . ."[44]

Too many times it has been said, not to be trite, but not nearly enough times considering how true it is—that the Lord God meant us to earn our way by our own effort. He could have made for us an effortless existence—*if* He hadn't known that growth and character and competence and satisfaction of soul come only with work—work that feeds and disciplines and develops and satisfies the spirit, the physical side, the mind and heart of man.

"The outlook for our country" wrote Irwin Edman, "lies in the quality of its idleness. . . ."[45] And to this we would add, in the quantity of its idleness also. And we can only say in gratitude, thank God for the blessing, for the right, for the privilege, for restoring, healing, peace-giving, satisfying—even for the blessed necessity—of useful, willing work.

The Morality of Work . . .

There is still another side of the subject of work that should be considered. For want of a better word we might call it the worthiness of work.

Work takes our time, and time is the very essence of life, and what we give our lives to is of incalculable consequence. And thus there could be little satisfaction, little justification, in unworthy work—work that would undermine men, that would mislead men's minds or their souls or their appetites—work that would in any way impair people.

Any time or effort or energy used to the detriment of men, any work which in purpose or in practice pulls men down physically or mentally or morally, probably isn't worthy work, regardless of whether it is profitable or politic or popular.

Work to deceive others, work to produce products that are not good for people, work to promote what is unwholesome, work to induce men to do what they should not do, to partake of what they should not partake, work to lead men into temptation, work that runs counter to the commandments, isn't worthy work.

On this question we would quote some sentences from a significant source: ". . . Whoever conceives labor in relationship to the divine purpose . . . will not lend his energies to the manufacture of goods which implicate [men] . . . in wicked and sinful activities. . . . The Christian is therefore bound to refuse to participate in the production of wicked and harmful items which injure or undermine the worth of man, as well as to refuse to buy them. . . . Nor can one reconcile . . . the expenditure of labor in the production of . . . worthless products. Drudgery in the production of worth-while articles may be justified, but . . ."[46] [not] "in the production of articles which have no real worth. There can be no sense of purpose in making trash"[47]—or, we might add, in working for what is of no worth.

The Lord God has said that "men should be anxiously engaged in a good cause"[48]—not merely "engaged," but engaged in "good." Working for the wrong things manifestly must be wrong. To be satisfying, to be acceptable, work must be more than merely motions, more than merely making money—it must be moral. Work should enlighten and lift life, and play its proper part in promoting the peace and health and happiness of people.

How We Work . . .

This we have said: that work should be more than merely motions; more than for money; it should also be moral—and since it is the expenditure of life itself, it should provide not only essential material substance, but also satisfaction and a real sense of service.

Now to the question of how we work: Work should be pursued if possible in an atmosphere of orderliness. We could scarcely imagine the Creator at work under distracting pressure or in other than orderliness. Nor can we believe that He would be hasty or harried or shoddy in His work— or do less than needed to be done, or fail to follow through. As the Father Himself set the example, so it was that His Son could say, "I have finished the work which thou gavest me to do."[49]

From another source we cite: "It was a blessing and not a curse; it was in mercy and not in wrath that man was commanded to eat his bread in the sweat of his face. . . . [work] is the fountain of all wealth, and of all happiness. Nations and individuals are alike utterly and entirely dependent upon it. . . . [In work] the destinies of the world are determined. . . ."[50]

The world needs the best effort of us all, and every person who does worthy, useful work, plays an important part—whether it is the doing of a household chore or the teaching of a child; the sewing of a button, or the building of a building.

People call us by the work we do. We are identified by the occupation or profession in which we are employed—and each person is entitled to the dignity, the pride, the honor of work, to a choice in his work, to the profit of work, to the worthiness, the orderliness, the artistry of work, and to a sense of service and sincere satisfaction—without too much pressure, but not too leisurely, not loafing, not holding back, not fearful of doing too much, not failing to give fair and full time. As someone pays for every hour, so is he entitled to fair effort and to a fair return.

As Ruskin wrote: ". . . work is only done well when it is done with a will; and no man has a thoroughly sound will unless he knows he is doing what he should, and is in his place. . . . not in a disorderly, scrambling, doggish way, but in an ordered . . . way. . . . Work is a thing done because it ought to be done, and with a determined end."[51]

". . . men *should* be anxiously engaged in a good cause, and do many things of their own free will, . . ."[48]—including good and worthwhile work.

Idleness and Inactivity

"The outlook for our country lies in the quality of its idleness. . . ."[45] To this we would add that the outlook of an individual lies in the quality of his idleness also.

There comes a time in the lives of those who live longer, when, for one reason or another, they must alter their activities. Things change, and people change, and personnel and procedures change. There is no man-made job that continues always and forever, and no earthly tenure that is unending. And those who live out the lengthening years of life always face the prospect of altered activities, and of a possible time of retirement.

Men vary from feeling that retirement is a hoped-for utopia to feeling that it is an intolerable inactivity. But a change of responsibilities does not mean that one should sit on the side lines. There is infinitely much undone. There is infintely much to be done. There is much need of mature judgment, mature emotions, of the experience and steadying leadership that those older can give to those younger.

One of the functions of the mature mind, said Maurice Linden, is "keeping alive human judgment, of maintaining human skills. . . ."[52] And it isn't reasonable to become accustomed to work and its great good, all the long length of life, and

[83]

then be altogether content without it. Whenever life is organized around idleness or inactivity, there is an emptiness. Life always asks of us a certain amount of flexibility, and inevitably it always asks of us adjustments to the changing years of time, but it does not ask of us the retirement to idleness, but only to altered activity.

"The old retain their intellectual powers provided their interests and inclination continue," said Cicero. "What one has, that one ought to use; . . . to each is allotted its appropriate quality . . . and so the feebleness of children, as well as the high spirit of youth, the soberness of mature years, and the ripe wisdom of . . . age—all have a certain natural advantage which should be (garnered) in its proper season."[53] And so long as a person feels useful, is useful and flexible and enjoys willing work—he is more likely to lengthen the health and happiness of his life.

The Waste of Doing
Only Average

We would preface these thoughts with a quotation from Carlyle: "Men do less than they ought, unless they do all that they can."[25] This suggests of course, the willingness to participate, the willingness to work, the willingness to use as fully as we can the gifts, the talents, the abilities, and the opportunities that the Lord God has given.

Some of us may waste time and opportunity by being fearful of doing too much. Some may impair capacity by holding back for fear of doing more than a fair share, by not wanting to do more than someone else does, by not wanting to exceed an average amount of effort or activity.

But we shouldn't let comparison with the average of others hold us back from being or doing our best. Capacity is increased by practice and performance; and if we hold our performance to the pace of the less able, or the less willing, or even to the average, we retard our own improvement; we impair our own capacity; and we impoverish ourselves, comparatively, and others also.

The Master's parable of the talents still presents one of the most basic lessons of life—for all the servants in the parable did not receive the same. But even though there was not an equality of endowment, there was seemingly an equality of accountability in that they all were judged by what they did with what they had.

We cannot reach our full powers or capacity if we are held back by the average, by the problem of comparative performance. The average is only what it is because some do more and some do less, and it is not in any sense an absolute or an ideal. And insofar as it would lead us to seek a lesser level, the worship of the average is false and futile.

All men and all things will only be raised as people are willing to improve performance. Again, in closing, we would quote Carlyle: "Men do less than they ought, unless they do all that they can."

"The Time That Is
Yet Thine..."

We are, all of us, a reflection of what we do with time, of what we want—or at least what we want enough to be willing to work for.

This, said William Penn—"this is ... said, that it might quicken, Thee, ... to lose none of the Time that is yet thine ... since without it we can do nothing in this World ... [and] God will certainly most strictly reckon with us, when Time shall be no more. . . ."[54]

"A purposeless life," said another quoted source, "is a life of fatigue. We all know from personal experience how tired we become while doing nothing, but once let us find an outlet for our energies, some object upon which to expand them, and our instinctive powers awake us to life. . . . None is so healthy and fresh as he who gives freely of his strength, and thereby liberates his impulses and instinctive powers into quickened activity."[55]

Often we have heard cited the scripture which says, "For as he thinketh in his heart, so is he."[56] As he thinketh not only so *is* he, but so *does* he— or is likely to do.

There is no mysterious formula for what man makes of his days on earth. Michelangelo said, "If people knew how hard I have had to work to gain my mastery, it would not seem wonderful at all."[57] So it is: In others we see the finished product, but we don't always see the process: the practice, the learning, the long labor, the giving up of other things, the arduous and seemingly almost endless endeavor.

To arrive at what we really want—or at what is really worth wanting—we must deeply desire, a desire that includes a dedicated pursuit of purpose, and not just a "wish it were." Wherever or whatever we want to be, we ought to be on our way— for time will go, and all there is of it is ours.

* * *

> "We will walk on our own feet; we will work with our own hands; we will speak our own minds . . ."[58]

—Emerson

"Thou Art What Thou Art"

"Thou art none the holier if thou art praised, nor the viler if thou art reproached. Thou art what thou art; . . ."[59]
—Thomas à Kempis

The Attitude of Intent . . .

We have read somewhere in some rules of safety the following sentence: "Never point a gun at anything you don't intend to shoot." This is basic to a whole series of parallel precautions essentially summarized in this single short sentence: "Don't start what you shouldn't do."

It applies to habits, to projects and promises, to attitudes and obligations, to every threat, every temptation, and to every intent.

The assumption that we can go a little way in the wrong way, that we can sin a little, lie a little, break the law a little; that we can be a little unfaithful, a little dishonest; or that we can start many things and stop them any time we want to, whenever and wherever we want to, without involvement, hurt, or harm, without falsely encouraging others, without being misunderstood, without the danger of going farther than we intended to go, is a false and unsafe assumption.

Those who find themselves in serious or embarrassing situations frequently say they didn't intend to do what they did. And often it is true that they didn't intend to go so far. But what is often also true is that they did entertain the idea, they did take the first step: they did make the problem possible. Like the man who points the gun, they assumed the attitude of intent.

Starting is so often easier than stopping. Habits are so often easier to acquire than they are to set aside. Relationships are often easier to begin than to break off. And we save ourselves much embarrassment, much explanation, much heartache, much danger, much tragedy if we simply don't start what we shouldn't do.

No one should flaunt any convention, invite any flirtation, or tempt any temptation, or begin a habit he wouldn't permanently want to have, or begin any relationship of life that would be unsafe or unsavory or unwise to follow through.

There is some scripture on the subject which says: "Abstain from all appearance of evil."[60] This also could be cited: "For as he thinketh in his heart, so is he."[56] Don't threaten anything you shouldn't follow through. Even would we say: Don't think to do anything you shouldn't do. Avoid not only the appearance of evil, but all invitation to it. In short, avoid the very attitude of intent. If you shouldn't, just don't do it.

"Seed and Fruit..."

To cite a sentence from Emerson: "Cause and effect, means and ends, seed and fruit, cannot be severed; . . ."[36] This suggests another sentence concerning cause and consequence which says, "There is a law, irrevocably decreed . . . upon which all blessings are predicated—And when we obtain any blessing . . . from God it is by obedience to that law upon which it is predicated."[61]

Sometimes slowly, sometimes swiftly, but always surely there *is* evidence of cause and consequence. The fruit *is* inseparable from the seed—which is its own assurance that nothing earned will ever be unfairly forfeited, that there will be justice in all we should or shouldn't do, in all we do or don't do, in every ultimate accounting.

This subject of seed and fruit has another side: the part thought plays in all utterance, in all action. To *think* of something unworthy may not be as wrong as to *do* something unworthy, but the thought does precede the deed, and more earnestly we should be careful what we contemplate and should safeguard every intent, for the deed, the act, is somewhat shaped long before the outward evidence, and what has not been held in the heart or in the mind, is less less likely to be done as a physical fact.

On the positive side there is this to say: Worthy,

clean, honest thinking is infinitely more likely to lead to clean and honest action. In one sense, good intentions have been much maligned. There is a place, it is said, that is paved with them. But good intentions are better than bad ones, even when we fail to follow them through. Better to have good ones neglected than bad ones accomplished!

And now for those who are young, for those who may look to life far to the future, there is this certainty of assurance: the willingness to study, to learn, to work, to keep clean in thought, in act, in utterance, the willingness to prepare and to be true to sound principles and purposes, the willingness to keep the commandments, brings peace and competence and quietness of conscience.

And as to the thoughts we think: Whatever leads to wrong must in itself be wrong. "The fruit is already in the seed"; the consequence is already in the cause, the inner intent comes to outward evidence. We cannot separate a person from what he thinks, from what he has in his heart. "When we obtain any blessing . . . it is by obedience to that . . . [principle] upon which it is predicated. . . ."[61] The "seed and fruit, cannot be severed."

What We Choose to Think...

Since thoughts are the forerunners of action, there sometimes comes the question: Where do thoughts come from? How can they be controlled?

It may sometimes be assumed that we are not responsible for the thoughts we think, since we cannot say for certain what might be their source. It is true that we little understand the mystery of memory, that we little understand the storing process of the mind, or how to erase impressions made upon the mind. And in idleness, and even in activity, random thoughts may come to immediate remembrance—in a manner for which we cannot account.

But it is also true in a positive sense that we can control our thoughts, we can control what we give our attention to. It requires the will, the wanting to, for the mind can surely wander far afield. But we can, if we will, make our minds consider a single subject; and we can, if we will, make our minds turn to another subject—not in vacancy, not in a void or vacuum, but by crowding out unwanted thoughts, by filling the channel with thoughts we want to think.

There is an old and trite saying, almost too trite to be quoted, but in principle profoundly true, that an idle mind is the devil's workshop. And even a busy mind can be the devil's workshop if it chooses or consents to concentrate on evil. It has been observed that the measure of a man is what he thinks when he doesn't have to think, what he thinks when he is alone, what he thinks in his idle hours.

No one would be so extreme as to say that it is possible never to have a stray or uninvited thought. But certainly we must say that we can choose to think certain things, we can choose to think of certain subjects. Thinking can, in large measure, be controlled, and the more we think clean, constructive, useful, moral thoughts, the more the mind makes channels that lead to high-minded habits.

Our thoughts are the evidence of our plans and purposes, the blueprints of what we propose, and it isn't safe to hold wrong thinking in the heart; it isn't safe to entertain evil.

The Lord God gave men the right to choose, the obligation to choose, the ability to choose, and it is the obligation of us all to choose such thoughts as would be safe and wise to follow through. There is no real way of separating ourselves from responsibility for our own thoughts and acts and utterances.

Control ... of Thought, of Action, of Utterance ...

Controlling thoughts is essential to controlling all we are ever likely to become, everything we are about to be. And he who persists in saying that he cannot help what he thinks, is in effect saying that he cannot help what he does. And if he cannot help what he thinks or what he does, he obviously could not be trusted under any conceivable circumstances.

But fortunately we can control thoughts, because we can choose to think other thoughts, and the obligation for choosing clearly is ours, but it does require will; it does require wanting to; it requires concentration. And this brings us to another side of the subject—the use of the mind for positive purposes.

Perhaps we have all been aware of being physically present and mentally absent. No doubt, we have all sat in classrooms or assemblies or been at social functions—apparently present. We were seen; we occupied space; we got credit on a roll book; we sat and looked and seemed to listen, but with the mind far afield. It is little that we learn unless we bring our awareness with us, unless we earnestly give attention, unless we discipline ourselves to think, to remember, to follow through.

But we can, if we will, concentrate; we can, if we will, make our minds consider a single subject; and we can, if we want to, make our minds turn to another subject.

In school, for example, we can think of chemistry at one period and of calculus at another. We *can* turn our attention to a particular train of thought at a particular time. And the answer to acquiring knowledge, to developing talent, to improving skills, is to choose to think what we should think, to choose to pursue constructive purposes, and not to be physically present and mentally absent.

"What we shall be, we are becoming," says an old proverb. We ought to be what we ought to be, and where we ought to be, and to be doing what we ought to be doing, and becoming what we ought to become—and the right to choose and to be responsible for our choice, is a responsibility that the Lord God has given. We need always to understand that we have to control ourselves, our thoughts, our actions, our utterances, and our every intent. What much more is a man except what he is inside himself.

"... to Think as He Ought ..."

Further as to the thoughts we think, and our responsibility for all our actions and utterances: This whole subject seems somehow to be summarized in a single sentence from Pascal, who said: "Man is obviously made to think. It is his whole dignity and his whole merit; and his whole duty is to think as he ought."[62]

It follows, of course, that if he thinks as he ought he will do as he ought, for thought is the forerunner of all action and utterance.

It is the power to think, to reason, to choose, that sets man apart, that gives him his high destiny if he uses well what the Lord God has given. It is with our thoughts, and the physical fulfillment of our thoughts, that we are all writing our own record— a record which one eminent scientist has said "is written in indelible script in space and time."[63]

Of course we should not always or inordinately think the same things. (Obsessions can be as undesirable as too much trivia.) We all need diversity of thought, some relaxation, some change of pace, some leisure, but not so much that idle and evil thoughts are invited to enter in.

What we need, all of us, always, is control: self-control, self-discipline, control of thought, appetite, utterance, action; the control to turn our attention to what we want to turn it to, to what we ought to turn it to, with an awareness that we are making of ourselves what we shall be, that "what we are to be, we are becoming"[64]—which fact would plead the importance of controlling self; of turning to the positive and purposeful use of life, of mind, time, talent; of directing to right ways the whole intent of the heart—of thinking what we ought to think, and refusing to resign to wrong ways.

"Man is obviously made to think. It is his whole dignity and his whole merit; and his whole duty is to think as he ought."[62]

"Other Things Being Equal..."

To the ever recurring question of judging others, of the power to appraise the motives, the actions, the intent of other people, we sometimes hear applied the phrase "other things being equal," or the phrase "under the same circumstances."

In physical factors this would seem to be so. We can weigh weights; we can measure measures; we can calculate speed and temperature and time and make things seem to be "equal under the same circumstances." But it isn't so easy to weigh people personally—as to the intangibles. It isn't so easy to know what's inside; in the mind, the heart, the spirit, what goes into the making of a man.

Experiences are not equal. Environments are not equal. The attitudes and influence and example of others are not equal in their impact upon us. Furthermore we arrived in the world at different times, with different talents and different opportunities.

". . . We do have a suspicion," as William Feather has said, "that it is nearly impossible for any body to put himself in another's place. Who is this man who asks you to put yourself in his place? . . . The differences are endless. . . ."[65] ". . . hence," added another observer, "the constant use of parables in our Saviour's teaching, that we might always be taught to turn from the letter to the spirit; . . . hence the persistent command to look from the outward to the inward, . . . from the act to the motive, from external, particular words and deeds to the character as a whole, from the things which are seen to the things which are unseen. . . ."[66]

William Penn has thus said in summary: ". . . the true Spring of the Actions of Men is as Invisible as their Hearts; . . ."[67] There must be laws; there must be rules. There must be enforcing of the laws and rules. And those who are called upon to judge cannot escape the doing of their sincere duty. But the longer we live, the closer we must come to know how hasty and wrong mere men can be in their estimate of others, and that the spirit is inseparable from the letter of the law. And it is comforting to know that, ultimately, the great just Judge of all of us will take all things into account, and will not err in measuring the man.

Inseparable from Ourselves...

From Horace we recall a comment quoted by Montaigne: "Reason and sense remove anxiety, Not houses that look out upon the sea. Why should we move to find countries and climates of another kind? What exile leaves himself behind?"[68]

Constantly, ceaselessly, we are keeping company with ourselves. Inseparably we live with ourselves, with our own thoughts, whether they are deep or shallow, clean or unclean, happy or unhappy—which suggests the great importance of learning, of repenting, of improving, of becoming more acceptable within ourselves.

When someone observed that a certain person did not appear to be much improved by his travels, Socrates said: "I very well believe it, for he took himself along with him."[69]

"We owe to our first journeys," observed Emerson, "the discovery that place is nothing. At home I dream that at Naples, at Rome, I can be intoxicated with beauty and lose my sadness. I pack my trunk, embrace my friends, embark on the sea and at last wake up in Naples, and there beside me is the stern Fact, the sad self, unrelenting, identical that I fled from. . . . Nothing can bring you peace but yourself."[70] Montaigne further added "We carry our fetters along with us: . . . we must . . . regain possession of ourselves."[71] And Caleb Colton referred to "traveled bodies, but untraveled minds."[72]

The so-called broadening influences are broadening only if there is a base that can be broadened. This doesn't only pertain to travel, but also to education, to art, to attitudes, to the learning of all the lessons of life. Not only is the impression important, but also the substance upon which the imprint is impressed. There must be character and capacity and purpose and principle, and solid substance within ourselves, and a clean and comfortable conscience, "For as he thinketh in his heart, so is he,"[56] and as his soul is inside him, so shall be his most constant companion. And our endless and earnest aim always, wherever we are, should be to have a self-respecting relationship with ourselves inside.

*　*　*

"The key to every man is his thought."[73]
　　　　　　　　　　　　　—Emerson

Some Essential Qualities of Character

"I have seldom known any one who deserted truth in trifles, that could be trusted in matters of importance."[74]

—William Paley

The Meaning of Honor . . .

We recall a comment accredited to Thomas Carlyle: "Conviction is worthless unless it is converted into conduct."[75] With this in mind we turn to the meaning of *honor,* without which there isn't much that is of worth in the world. We are not speaking of titles given, or positions held, or of honors conferred, but of the honor that is inseparably a part of a person inside himself.

Honor, honorable, honesty: these are associated with some other solid and wonderful words: trust, integrity, truth; courage, character, conscience, and high conduct; dignity, respect, and respectability; keeping credit, paying debts when due; purity, chastity, virtue; sincerity, decency, faithfulness; freedom from fraud, freedom from guile, freedom from duplicity and deception. These solid words are all associataed with honor, honorable, honesty. And unless, as Carlyle said, they are converted into conduct, a man is not safe in his person or in his property, in anything he buys or sells, in any contract or commitment, or in any trust or treaty.

Honor is more than mere legality; more than the letter of the law; more than position, than reputation, than some kinds of success or public acceptance. It is not a matter of what is known or not known, what one can get away with, or what is popular or profitable or politic. It is freedom from deceit, from evil thinking, from evil intent; freedom from fraud. It is what makes it possible for a person to rely on what he reads or sees or hears, to rely on a label. It is what makes a woman or a girl or an innocent child safe. It is not promises, but performance.

It is simply a matter of whether something is or isn't so. It is character and "conviction," as Carlyle said, "converted into conduct"—without which there is little of worth in the world.

The Quality of Courage . . .

"Whatever you do," said Emerson, "you need courage. Whatever course you decide upon, there is always someone to tell you you are wrong. There are always difficulties arising which tempt you to believe that your critics are right. To map out a course of action and follow it to an end requires . . . courage. . . ."[76]

There is no significant decision of life that doesn't require some sort of courage, and no typical day of life that doesn't require some sort of courage; and certainly there is no great venture in life that doesn't require courage. "Courage is the greatest of all the virtues. Because if you haven't courage, you may not have an opportunity to use any of the others."[77] It takes courage to be different. It takes courage to side with someone who is being unfairly abused. It takes courage to befriend someone who is in popular disfavor, to advocate an unpolitic or unprofitable opinion. It takes courage to speak out in favor of an unpopular proposal, or an inconvenient or unpopular principle. It takes courage to turn down a dare. It takes courage to ignore derision, even when one is right. Sometimes it takes courage even to run away from an evil proposal, for evil, like misery, loves company, and doesn't make it easy for anyone to run out on it.

Often it takes courage to find the peace that

comes with repenting. Pursuing anything that isn't easy, isn't popular, anything that isn't soon successful, requires courage. The critics are often cruel, sometimes honestly sometimes for reasons that are other than honest. Sometimes they are right; sometimes they are wrong. But anyone who stands for anything, who says anything, who does anything that amounts to much, must face the critics—and that requires courage.

"Whatever you do, you need courage"—especially the courage that comes with a conviction of right—and the equal, or even almost greater, courage to repent from wrong. Life itself, with its every significant decision, requires courage.

The Quality of Kindness

In the observations of an eminent British industrialist we find some comments on the quality of kindliness: "Next I think I would choose kindness in its widest sense. Not, please not, either the hail-fellow-well-met or the do-gooding that too often goes by the name of kindness, but in its real and true sense of active love for one's fellow men, the sort of kindness that contains within itself generosity of mind and spirit, courtesy and good temper."[78]

This suggests some simple lines by an author whose name we do not know:

> "I have wept in the night
> For the shortness of sight
> That to somebody's need made me blind;
> But I never have yet
> Felt a tinge of regret
> For being a little too kind."[11]

Everything that is accomplished in life, personally and professionally, publicly and privately, is affected by personal qualities of character, including the quality of kindliness. Discipline is essential at times; facts must be faced. But *how* things are done is often equally important with *what* is done. *How* things are said is often equally important with *what* is said. A comment can be critical and kind or critical and unkind—constructive or destructive.

Life has its problems for all, its days of discouragement, its sorrows, its difficulties and disappointments; but much bitterness and heartbreak can be softened by the quality of kindliness, which *includes* sincere consideration, and which *excludes* cruel or cutting sarcasm, ridicule, and every intent to embarrass, to insult, to degrade.

Kindness should be cultivated in all relationships of life: between parents and children; brothers and sisters; teachers and students; neighbor to neighbor; and every man to every other. The quality of kindliness is in part the essence of the message of the Master of mankind, with love and peace and respect for people.

> "O the kind words we give shall in memory live
> And sunshine forever impart;
> Let us oft speak kind words to each other;
> Kind words are sweet tones of the heart."[79]

Integrity—Without Side Considerations

The subject of integrity suggests itself for consideration. The words associated with it are themselves reassuring: ". . . the quality of being complete, . . . unbroken—unimpaired—moral soundness, purity, honesty, freedom from corrupting influence or practice, strictness in the fulfillment of contracts . . . and in the discharge of trusts."

This is the quality that gives assurance that, as things seem to be, they are; that an endorsement represents an honest judgment, and not merely an opinion paid for.

In a simple forthright sentence, Washington said: "I hope I shall always possess firmness and virtue enough to maintain what I consider the most enviable of all titles, the character of an honest man."[80]—and Alexander Pope added: "An honest man's the noblest work of God."[81] Herbert Spencer said: "Not education, but character, is man's greatest need and man's greatest safeguard."[82] ". . . Young Washington resolved to adhere absolutely to truth," wrote Douglas Southall Freeman, "to practice rigid honesty, to do his full duty, to put forth his largest effort, to maintain uniform courtesy and, above all, to deal justly."[83]

[113]

In this he may have left us our greatest heritage; or at least he left us an example of a quality of character we must have, if we are to preserve the heritage we have.

Surely there is no greater need for our time than the need for integrity, for being true to trust, being assured that the whole substance of things can be seen from the top of the table. And this is not something that new laws or legislation will fix, or new rules or regulations, for ingenious men will always find ways to circumvent both laws and locks.

Integrity is simply something that a man is within himself. It is, in a sense, the assurance that what one sees, what something seems, what should be, what is said to be, is something that can be counted on, without side considerations.

The Quality of Sincerity

In considering some essential qualities of character, a British industrialist had this to say of sincerity: "I am as certain as one can be, . . that a great deal of any absence of industrial goodwill from which we may be suffering, and to go even farther, of our industrial unrest, is due to the fact that we have failed time and time again to convince each other of our sincerity and honesty of intention and purpose."[78]

This sentence suggests, among other things, that sincerity is simply honesty of intent. The dictionary also suggests some significant synonyms: "straightforward, honest, free from hypocrisy, being in reality what appears to be; genuine, true, real; not falsely assumed; authentic, correct, frank, unfeigned, unaffected."

Sincerity does not necessarily have anything to do with politeness or polish or politics or policy—but should add its own element of honesty to any or all of these. It is more than conversation; more than front; more than passing pleasantries. It is doing what one says. It is meaning what one says. It is not presenting the face of friendship yet lacking the loyalty. It is what gives a person assurance that his interests are safe in his absence when someone assures him that it will be so. It is being truly interested when we ask someone how he is.

It is meaning it when we ask someone to let us know if we can help. It is what gives us something we can count on.

We would here quote Anne Morrow Lindbergh's comment that "the most exhausting thing in life, . . is being insincere"[84]—pretense—saying something that isn't so, or trying to make what isn't seem to be so. In all of life it is exceedingly essential to find the real facts, to see the real face.

Before God there can be no concealment or deception. And among men sincerity is an essential quality of character—the sincerity which is simply the assurance of honest intent.

The Quality of Loyalty

One quality of character that must not be overlooked is the quality of loyalty. It is essential in every worthy relationship of life: in families; among friends; between teammates; between employer and employee; loyalty to those who work for us, and with us, and loyalty to those who provide employment.

When we work for someone in honorable employment, we should give full service—for only by the success and solvency of the ventures we work for can there be assurance of security. And so long as we receive benefits from an honorable source we should be loyal to it, and contribute to its success.

Like other essential qualities of character, loyalty gives the assurance of what we can count on. It gives the assurance that friends will not faintheartedly fade from us at the first failure of fair weather. This does not mean that a person should protect another person in evil, or in violation of law, but should insist on fair presentation of facts. Significantly, a search would show that loyalty comes from the same word root as law, and these words are associated in dictionary definition: "Faithful and true to the lawful government . . . true to any person or persons to whom one owes fidelity, as a wife to her husband, friend to friend;

fidelity to a superior [and, we might add—to a subordinate] . . . to duty . . . to principle; . . . lawful and legitimate . . . allegiance."

This calls up the question of what might be called "unlawful loyalty." Lawless men may be loyal so long as their mutual safety or survival depends upon it, but disloyal as soon as one, by sacrificing the other, can serve the cause of his own safety or survival. One cannot enter into an evil or unlawful act or association, or conspire to do anything dishonorable with anyone else, and be assured of the limits of loyalty. Evil and friendship, evil and honor, are not compatible.

But the righteous love and loyalty of family and friends; loyalty among people for high purpose, loyalty to high principle—such is the loyalty that persuades a person to stand steadfast as to an issue or an honorable obligation, even after it becomes inconvenient. Without the quality of loyalty there is little in life that can be counted on.

Debt: a Real and Actual Obligation

Debt is a burden, a worry (or should be)—that is, it should be if it is a debt past due. Debt is a real and actual obligation. It represents the use of something that actually wasn't ours, or the use of something for which we have postponed payment. And it is a fallacy to feel that being somewhat deep in debt, it doesn't matter very much if we go yet deeper.

Here, in a sense, is a matter of repentance, a matter of reversing the process. No one in debt is likely to get out unless he does something different from that which got him into debt.

Of course, there is the unavoidable, the unexpected: the accidents, the illnesses, and other adverse events; and there is generally a disposition to be understanding of the necessary and the unavoidable. But basically borrowing carries with it the obligation of paying back.

Either we reduce obligations or we increase obligations, and credit is given with the expectancy that the debtor will reduce the debt. And respect and confidence and sound credit come with an honest attitude toward honoring obligations. Embarrassment and discomfort and the killing of confidence and credit come with ignoring or attempting to move out from under obligations.

No man is ever out of debt who always goes in deeper. No man is ever out of debt who always promises more than he pays. In this, as in other things also, the direction in which we move matters much. Because a man may be down deep doesn't mean that he should go down deeper. And this, or any other, is a season to resolve not needlessly or irresponsibly to go down deeper into debt.

A Summation: Qualities of Character

These qualities of character—faith, courage, kindness, integrity, sincerity, loyalty—all seem in a sense to add up to a simple word—a word which doesn't include them all, but without which all else would be of little use—and what they add up to is a kind of guilelessness, which is simply plain and simple honesty. The Psalmist said it in this sentence: "Blessed is the man unto whom the Lord imputeth not iniquity, and in whose spirit there is no guile."[85]

Now, for a summation, we turn to some sentences from three sources, the first consisting of some wise and ancient words from Marcus Antoninus, from back some eighteen centuries: "Do not consider anything for your interest which makes you break your word, quit your modesty, or inclines you to any practice which will not bear the light, or look the world in the face."[86]

Two others are cited from the eighteenth and nineteenth centuries: "In all things preserve integrity; and the consciousness of thine own uprightness will alleviate the toil of business, soften the hardness of ill-success and disappointments, and give thee an humble confidence before God, when the ingratitude of man, or the iniquity of

[121]

the times may rob thee of other reward."[73]

Now from the third source: "Give us a character on which we can thoroughly depend, which we know to be based on principle and on the fear of God, and it is wonderful how many [other] brilliant and popular and splendid qualities we can safely and gladly dispense with."[87]

Simply, this all adds up to being honest with ourselves, honest with others, honest with the Lord God, and honest in an endeavor to keep His commandments. Peace and confidence and love and loyalty lie in this direction; unhappiness and sorrow in any other. Despite all sophistries and cynicism this is simply so.

No person has the right to harm another (or himself, for that matter), or to take unjustly from another, to take the virtue of another, to impair the faith of another. And anyone who isn't honest is simply punishing himself; for there isn't any way to peace, or to happiness, or any real progress, or any lasting and satisfactory relationship in life without an absolute honesty—an honesty that is akin to a kind of guilelessness that knows no duplicity or deception, that knows no crafty cunning.

This in summary from a significant source: "The foundation of leadership is personal character, . . . Personal character . . . is in fact the prime determinant in . . . success or failure . . ."[78]

* * *

"Not education, but character, is man's greatest need and man's greatest safeguard."[82]

—Herbert Spencer

Self-Control, and Liberty, and Law...

"What is liberty without wisdom and without virtue?"[88]

—Edmund Burke

Self-control, and Liberty,
and Law . . .

We recall these two phrases from a moving and meaningful song: "Confirm thy soul in self-control, Thy liberty in law."[89]

Always and earnestly urgent in all the issues and in all the aspects of life are self-control and liberty and law. And always to be taught, and never to be forgotten, is that liberty is preserved by law. Self-control and liberty and law are basic to life, basic to the eternal plans and purposes of the Lord pertaining to his children. But sometimes we seem more to have remembered freedom than self-control, liberty more than the law.

As we come together, live together, as we serve and receive service in a world where physically we come ever closer together, always we have to have self-control, always we have to live our lives with law as well as with liberty. Always we have to consider the rights, the privileges, the comfort, the convenience of others, with an awareness that we have no right to do anything we want, to take anything we want, or irresponsibly to say anything we want, or to befoul the moral atmosphere, or the water others use, the air where others are, the peace that others have, or their rightful privacy, or to live uninhibited lives. We have to be considerate of others always. Self-control, with law, is the only safeguard of liberty; and not the existence of law only, but respect for law, obeying the law—the laws of God, the laws of the land.

In a meaningful commencement address a great American said this of laws and liberty not many months before he left this life: "We are too inclined," he said "to think of law as something merely restrictive—something hemming us in. We sometimes think of law as the opposite of liberty. But that is a false conception . . . God does not contradict Himself. He did not create man and then, as an afterthought, impose upon him a set of arbitrary, irritating, restrictive rules. He made man free—and then gave him the commandments to keep him free. . . . We cannot break the Ten Commandments. We can only break ourselves against them—or else, by keeping them, rise through them to the fulness of freedom under God. God means us to be free. With divine daring, He gave us the power of choice."[90]

To this great utterance we would add: The greatest threat to liberty is lawlessness. And the greatest assurance of liberty is respect for law. "Confirm thy soul in self-control, Thy liberty in law."

Obeying, Honoring, and Sustaining the Law

In considering the importance of law in our lives, we would preface what follows with this simple yet profound fact: that obeying, honoring, and sustaining the law is basic to all peace, all progress, and to the safety and security of all people and all property.

Nature obeys law; the universe obeys law; and men, for their safety and survival and for the salvation of their souls, must obey law. And there is nothing perhaps of much more importance pertaining to young people than to set before them an example of respect for law, of the living of law —an example on the part of parents, of teachers, and all others in honoring and sustaining law. Indeed, laxity toward law can lead to the loss of much that is most dear in life.

Sometimes the young—and others also—resent restraint. They hear of freedom and forget that freedom can only be preserved by the living of law. If everyone were lawless everyone would be bound by fear, would have to live by force, and no one would be secure in his life, his property, or his possessions—for the absence of respect for law leads to looseness and license. The absence of law is anarchy, and anarchy has never worked in the world. ". . . That which is governed by law is also preserved by law. . . ."[91]

These facts, among many others, suggest in summary: first, that the law should be as simple and understandable as possible; second, that law should be lived, honored, observed; and that parents and all others also should set before the young, an example of living and respecting law, from the earliest years of youth—an example that the young may safely look to for their attitudes toward law and life, for law is the safeguard of life, and he who flaunts it is endangering his own rights, his own freedom, his own safety and survival.

"There is a law, irrevocably decreed in heaven before the foundations of this world, upon which all blessings are predicated—And when we obtain any blessing . . . it is by obedience to that law upon which it is predicated."[61] Restraint and self-control are two essentials in the living of the law, and are of prime importance among all the lessons of life.

On Understanding Freedom

As days of patriotic observance come and go, there is much said concerning freedom. Like all other principles which affect men, freedom in theory may be one thing and freedom in practice may be quite another. It is a term comparatively easy to define academically, but sometimes difficult to define in the everyday relationships of life, because men have so many different ideas of freedom, and so many misconceptions concerning it.

There are some, for example, who are committed to the principle of freedom for everyone and others who want it only for themselves. It is they who have forgotten that no man's freedom is safe, so long as any man is in bondage.

Then there are those who want freedom to abuse their freedom—who want complete license, freedom from all restraint, from the necessary disciplines of life, from law and order. It is they who mistake anarchy for freedom.

All of us, of course, want our freedom to complain and to criticize. We may not always use this freedom, but without it we are not free.

And then there are some of us who expect not only freedom but also a free living. But there is a great difference. Freedom must include freedom to work but not freedom from work. Freedom from want without effort may sound like Utopia, but

[129]

actually is a false and empty freedom.

There are many other so-called freedoms which some of us may think we want, but which no straight-thinking man actually does want when he understands where they lead. Among these are freedom from responsibility, from troubling ourselves with the issues of the day—and even freedom from thinking for ourselves. But when we indulge such freedoms we do so at great cost, because he who does not carry his share of the burdens of his own day and generation cannot long expect to have the blessings of freedom—and he who does not think for himself is never free.

God be thanked for freedom, for, with all it is abused, and neglected, and misunderstood, anything for which we could exchange it would be a bad bargain!

"The American Constitution..."

The words of the great British statesman, William E. Gladstone, suggest a subject: ". . . the American Constitution, is so far as I can see, the most wonderful word ever struck off at a given time by the brain and purpose of man."[92] And we would cite also from another source: "The Constitution of the United States is a glorious standard; . . . a heavenly banner; . . . like the cooling shades and refreshing waters of a great rock in a weary and thirsty land . . . . like a great tree under whose branches men from every clime can be shielded from the burning rays of the sun . . . founded in the wisdom of God"[93] "by the hands of wise men whom [God] raised up unto this very purpose."[94]

With the recurring anniversary of the Constitution, the contrast between the principle of freedom and the opposite intent to enslave men and their minds has become so sharp, so apparent, that gratitude for freedom and dedication to its principles and preservation could scarcely be over-emphasized. In a recent significant address an eminent judge had this to say concerning these contrasts: ". . . today we face a crisis which calls upon the devotion of every citizen as never before . . . funds have been poured out like water . . . for the preservation of freedom. . . . But material benefits are not enough, we must keep the flame of freedom burning . . . teach the youth coming on the meaning of the Declaration of Independence, of the Constitution of the United States" and "create in the uncaptured nations a love of liberty like that which led our fathers to cross the seas . . . The oppressed should also know that the choice is not mainly between low and high standards of living, but between freedom and slavery. . . ."[95]

The following is from the words of Washington: ". . . it is easy to foresee," he said, "that, from different causes, and from different quarters, much pains will be taken, many artifices employed, to weaken in your mind the conviction of this truth . . . against which the batteries of internal and external enemies will be most constantly and actively (though often covertly and insidiously) directed." And you must watch "for its preservation with jealous anxiety."[96] And this from Andrew Jackson: "Our Constitution is no longer a doubtful experiment . . . It has . . . shown the wisdom and foresight of those who framed it; . . . You have the highest of human trusts committed to your care. Providence has showered on this favored land blessings without number, and has chosen you, as the guardians of freedom, to preserve it for the benefit of the human race. May he who holds in his hands the destinies of nations make you worthy of the favors he has bestowed, and enable you, with pure hearts, and pure hands, and sleepless vigilance, to guard and defend to the end of time the great charge he has committed to your keeping."[97]

"How Much Is All This Worth? ..."

Many years ago Daniel Webster recalled a question: "How much is all this worth?"[98] As to liberty, or the lack of it, whatever the price, it is priceless, and the difference cannot be calculated.

How much is it worth to live where one wishes? to work at what one wishes? to worship as one wishes? How much is it worth to have the right to live with loved ones? to listen to the laughter of children? to be unafraid of approaching footsteps? to walk home and find the welcome of loved faces unafraid?

How much is it worth to own personal property? to have personal privacy? How much is it worth to preserve human dignity? How much is it worth to choose leaders? to vote in an open and honest election? to have a voice in making and administering the laws of the land?

How much is it worth to come and to go, to live and to choose, to think and to speak, to read and to search? to have an education offered everyone? How much is it worth freely to express an opinion, fearlessly to move from place to place, with an openness of life, a free ranging of the mind; and enjoyment of the great and goodly earth

[133]

that God has given, with peace of mind and quiet conviction?

Despite all encroachments on freedom, and all unwise relinquishment of some rights, still blessed beyond belief, still precious beyond price, is the freedom our forebears paid for—the freedom which is God-given, which yet, paradoxically, has to be everlastingly earned and deserved over and over again, and can never safely be permitted to become commonplace.

How much is all this worth? All this must be worth the willingness to work, to defend, to give allegiance, to be a participating partner, to live with honor, justice, and respect for law, and the willingness to keep the commandments—for "No free government," wrote Andrew Jackson, "can stand without virtue in the people and a lofty spirit of patriotism: . . ."[97]

Thank God for liberty and for the privilege of preserving it at any price.

* * *

"There are two freedoms, the false where one is free to do what he likes, and the true where he is free to do what he ought."[99]

—Charles Kingsley

Happiness, Comparisons, and a Quiet Conscience

"Happiness is not a reward—it is a consequence."[100]

—Robert G. Ingersoll

Happiness—and the Paradox of Comparison

A sentence written some two or more centuries ago is significant in the search for the happiness that all of us so much seek. "If one only wished to be happy," it says, "this could be easily accomplished; but we wish to be happier than other people, and this is always difficult, for we believe others to be happier than they are."[6]

This suggests, of course, that the comparative element always enters in—that we are happy or unhappy merely by comparison with other people, with what others are or aren't, with what others have or haven't. This paradox is both fact and fallacy, because for happiness there must be some set standards, some basic essentials. Yet neither can we quite keep out comparisons.

In the later years of World War II, the latest models of many things were old and outdated by present comparisons. Yet if we had the latest, we felt comparatively pleased—until later and better things again began to be. Then what we had was soon again not good enough.

This is not necessarily a negative quality of character. We ought to want progress and improvement. We ought, in a reasonable way, to want not only the better but the best. A controlled, intelligent discontent is a constructive quality of character, and a complete complacency is a negative quality of character.

But if we make ourselves unhappy or run ourselves deeply into debt or restlessly run from place to place, simply for comparative purposes, we shall not be likely to find the peace, the happiness, the contentment, the accomplishment we so much seek. And when the discontent of wanting something is with us, we should be sure it is something worth wanting.

We should be discontented with ignorance. We should seek wisdom, understanding, seek learning, "even by study and also by faith."[101] We should seek improvement both of mind and of matter, and be grateful for gifts and talents and opportunities and all the Lord God has given. But because we can't be everything that everyone else is, or have everything that everyone else has, we should not brood about it. Nobody has everything that everybody else has.

To conclude with our opening quote: "If one only wished to be happy, this could be easily accomplished; but we wish to be happier than other people, and this is always difficult, for we believe others to be happier than they are."[6]

Goodness and Greatness

In the magnifying of so much that is mediocre some words are often overworked—like *great* and *greatness,* for example, and associated synonyms. Yet the true quality of greatness is often found in unpublicized places, in simple, modest settings, in the heroic lives of humble men and women—the greatness of goodness and of sincere service.

"Goodness is richer than greatness," said Edwin Hubbel Chapin. "It lifts us nearer to God . . . . It is . . . manifested according to our abilities, within our sphere, . . . and every day I bless God that the great necessary work of the world is so faithfully carried on by humble men in narrow spaces and by faithful women in narrow circles, . . . performing works of simple goodness . . . ."[102] Everywhere sincere and unassuming people are performing sincere and essential service, day by day, year by year, doing their share, carrying their sorrows, caring for their own, helping others, doing much that is greatly good.

"Not a day passes over the earth but men and women of no note do great deeds, speak great words, and suffer noble sorrows"—said another source—"of these obscure heroes, . . . the greater part will never be known till that hour when many

[139]

that were great shall be small and the small great."[103]

There is greatness in service where there is sickness, often under disheartening circumstances. There is greatness in enduring disappointments, in meeting obligations; greatness in work earnestly and honestly done.

There is greatness in teaching, greatness in trying, in trusting, greatness in patient waiting.

There is greatness in understanding, in forgiving, in repenting.

There is greatness—a very great kind of greatness—in self-control, in tempering appetite, in tempering temper.

There is greatness in cleanliness of life, in keeping faith, in keeping the commandments.

"Greatness . . . [is] not so much a certain size as a certain quality in human lives . . . ."[104] And what is not good is not great, no matter how glamorous or desirable it sometimes seems. As Samuel Johnson said it: "Nothing can be truly great which is not right."[105]

Thank God for heroic greatness in humble lives, in humble hearts and homes, greatness in devotion, in faithfulness, in being true to trust, in the simple doing of duty—a kind of greatness which the Lord God will not forget.

"What Exile Leaves Himself Behind?"

It is apparent that at times the pressures of life are upon us all. Anxieties, difficulties, decisions —even opportunities weigh heavily under some circumstances. And, collectively, we meet pressures and problems in many ways. We sometimes ignore them or seek to evade them. We sometimes face them full in the face, with the faith to know that, as we do what we can, help and strength come from sources both inside and outside ourselves.

Certainly one of the least likely ways of solving any situation satisfactorily is by refusal to face facts. In one of his writings Montaigne implied the ineffectiveness of trying to evade issues—of trying, in a sense, to run away from ourselves or our obligations or our opportunities, and from Horace he quoted the classic language of this lesson: "Reason and sense remove anxiety, Not houses that look out upon the sea. Why should we move to find countries and climates of another kind? What exile leaves himself behind?"[68] When, indeed, did anyone ever leave himself behind?

There are times when all of us need a change of pace, rest and recreation, and time to step aside and think things through. But no one *ever* leaves *himself* behind. And changes—repentance, the altering of attitudes, the meeting of problems and of opportunities, and all personal improvement, these have to happen inside ourselves, in addition to whatever help we may receive from other sources.

We must move on from wherever we are, knowing that there are problems and decisions, consequences and compensations in all endeavors—that there are scars of battle, in a sense, in all we undertake to do—and that life isn't altogether easy for anyone.

We have to learn to live through; to hold on; to believe; to try; to trust. And peace comes— personal peace—with the courage to repent, to improve upon the past, to meet the problems and opportunities of the present, and to have faith in the future.

"Reason and sense remove anxiety, Not houses that look out upon the sea. Why should we move to find countries and climates of another kind? What exile leaves himself behind?"

On "Desensitizing Ourselves"

We have spoken of the person as being of greater importance than the place, and of our being inseparable from ourselves, which means, in a measure, that no matter where we are or who we are or what we are or how much help we have, we have to do some part of the solving of our problems for ourselves. We have to have the will and the willingness inside ourselves.

And this we say in face of the fact that there sometimes seems to be a tendency to desensitize people in a sense, physically, morally, mentally— sometimes almost seeming to be a seeking to evade rather than a seeking to solve.

We have quoted the comment concerning seeking "countries and climates of another kind,"[68] which is in many ways wonderful, *if* it doesn't expect too much of the place and too little of the person. Seeking to escape routine and reality may, in moderation, be desirable, but overdone, could seem to cause some question—as, for example, when people perennially play at play harder than they work at work. Yet work itself is one of life's surest satisfactions and one of its surest shock absorbers.

And now to another side of the subject: In the search for evasion there is sometimes a resorting to the use of substances which lead to a dulling of the senses, the dulling of thinking, of judgment, the dulling of physical reflexes—and even the dulling of the acuteness of conscience. "There is nothing that a man can less afford to leave at home," said Richardson Packe, "than his conscience or his good habits."[106] To which we would add, there is nothing that he can less afford to reduce to lower level, by any means, than his conscience, his good habits, or his sense of real responsibility for his own actions.

The Lord God gave us an awareness of ourselves: physically and mentally and spiritually—and that which he gave us should not be abused, or reduced to a lower level. He expects of us a reasonable effort, a reasonable use of talents and intelligence and opportunities, a reasonable self-control, a reasonable meeting of every hour. He expects of us an earnest, patient doing, and enduring, and a reconciliation with reality, and not, generally speaking, too much lowering of our awareness or, in a sense, the desensitizing of ourselves.

"There is nothing that a man can less afford to leave . . . [behind] than his conscience or his good habits."

On Being Better...

No doubt most of us are aware of things we should like to altar in our own lives, in the lives of others, and in the whole outlook of events; and often we are kept going by our faith and hope that there will come a time when things will be better.

Often we wish for a time when we ourselves shall be better, when we shall be personally improved, when our affairs will be in better order, when we shall do and be and act more as we would want to. But when we are dissatisfied with ourselves or with circumstances, or when we are not making progress along our intended path, our hope should be more than merely hope.

Sometimes we hope to have more friends, but the friends we hope to have come from being the kind of friend we wish others were. We may hope for our debts to be paid. But debts don't dissolve themselves by our piling more debts upon them, or by leaving them as they are. We have no real reason to hope for debts to disappear or for conditions to be better if we do nothing to make them better.

Sometimes we are carried toward consequences beyond our control by uninvited events that take us where we do not choose to go. But we don't always have to accept ourselves or circumstances

[145]

outside ourselves as they are. There are many day-to-day decisions which we can in a measure make and must make which would give us more real reason to hope for a finer future.

And it should be said again and again that we shall not suddenly become something we are not. The building process, personal progress and improvement, and the power to do better and be better, don't just suddenly come without effort. The only way to repent is to repent. The only way to improve is to improve. The only way to be what we want to be is to begin to be what we ought to be. We cannot alter the trend of the past or improve upon the present simply by sitting as we are or by continuing down a wrong road.

The Light "Which Lighteth Every Man"

It is recorded in the first book of the Bible that God said: "Let there be light" (Gen. 1:3)—and from there on through scripture, the great theme of light is over and over emphasized:

"The Lord is my light" (Ps. 27:1); "Let us walk in the light of the Lord" (Isa. 2:5); "Then shall thy light break forth" (Isa. 58:8); "Arise, shine, for thy light is come" (Isa. 60:1); "Ye are the light of the world" (Matt. 5:14); "a burning and a shining light" (John 5:35); "Let your light so shine before men" (Matt. 5:16); "Walk as children of light" (Eph. 5:8); "Christ shall give thee light" (Eph. 5:14); "a light that shineth in a dark place" (II Pet. 1:19).

Among all these (and many more) is one not yet mentioned, found in the first chapter of John, which speaks of the true light "which lighteth every man that cometh into the world" (John 1:9).

Men do come into the world with a light implanted within them—a light that gives them inherently some discrimination between right and wrong, some response to good, some revulsion against evil.

It is true that many laws and manners are man-made. But the timeless virtues, the eternal truths, the ageless questions of right and wrong are not man-made. As to conscience: It is true that children must be taught the fundamentals of right and wrong. But it is also true that no matter what men are or are not taught, there is implanted within them something besides custom and convention and man-made manners. Even a man who hasn't been taught to have an acute conscience is not happy if the course of his life is running against the light.

Men are sincerely, wholesomely happy, and at peace in their innermost hearts only as they allow themselves to be led by light—the light that is implanted within, the light that leads to truth, "the light which lighteth every man that cometh into the world," and that leads to further light.

"A Still and Quiet Conscience"

We would turn for a moment or two to the question of a quiet conscience, which is in a sense, simply self-respect, the real respect that comes with being free from the inward accusation that surely follows offenses.

J. A. Petit-Senn, more than a century ago, said, "A good conscience never costs as much as it is worth."[107] Shakespeare said it in this sentence: "I feel within me a peace above all earthly dignities, A still and quiet conscience."[108] And Austin Phelps added: "A disciplined conscience is a man's best friend.—It may not be his most amiable, but it is his most faithful monitor."[109] And from Joseph Addison comes this comment, "A good conscience is to the soul what health is to the body; it preserves constant ease and serenity within us, . . ."[110] And from Sir Walter Raleigh, ". . . the justice of God doth require none other accuser than our own consciences. . . ."[111]

To these we would add two short citations from the Epistles of Paul: "Pray for us: for we trust we have a good conscience, in all things willing to live honestly."[112] And ". . . finally, brethren, whatsoever things are true, whatsoever things are honest, whatsoever things are just, whatsoever things are pure, . . . think on these things."[113]

All this may sound to some like a citation of

platitudes and of old-fashioned axioms, but such factors are indispensable to all satisfactory personal and professional and public relationships in life—and to the whole working of the world. (And, parenthetically, whatever pertains to the public pertains to people personally.)

Without the basic virtues no one can continue confidently to do business with anyone else, nor can anyone find peace or abiding satisfaction inside himself. And what sometimes seems impractical or idealistic, proves, in fact, to be the only practical or workable relationship between men and between the organizations they create to front for them.

Despite all the cynical may say, there is always the irrevocable accounting a man keeps inside himself—and honesty and fairness and freedom from offense are essential to a quiet conscience and to sincere self-respect.

* * *

"Conscience is the voice of the soul."[114]
—Jean Jacques Rousseau

Of Faith and Peace
and Repentance

"Let us correct our errors forward, not backward."[115]

—Henri Bergson

"What We Are to Be, We Are Becoming..."

When we have done wrong things, when we have thought wrong thoughts, when we have made mistakes, we can well be exceedingly grateful for the great and blessed principle of repentance—because there isn't very much that anyone can do about the past, except to learn from it. But there is much we can do about the present and the future.

John Locke said, ". . . men from their youth . . . let a good part of their lives run uselessly away, . . ."[16] One of the most useless ways of wasting life comes with supposing that because we *have* wasted it or *have* misused it, or *have* done something that was unworthy, it is useless to turn toward a right way. Sometimes we may suppose that the pattern is so set that it is useless to try to change. But who is qualified to say when it is useless to change, to repent, to improve, when it is useless to turn from a wrong way?

No man is justified in assuming that there is no further point in repentance; no man is justified in assuming that there is no possibility of improving. Any improvement in any degree, in any circumstance or situation, any turning to the better is all to the good, and there is no point in postponement.

Indeed, there is great fallacy in those who suppose that because they have done some wrong they must resign themselves to wrong. There is no justification ever at any time for anyone to resign himself to wrong. No matter how far a person has persisted on a contrary course, there is no reason why he should continue on such a course one step more or one moment more. The turning back is hard: the remorse that must be felt; the pride that must be set aside; the admitting of mistakes. But there is always good reason for turning from a wrong way.

While penalties are always paid for wrong, repentance is the only hope we have—and to cite again this quoted sentence: "I believe . . . we will be judged as we are, for what we are, and maybe not for what we have been!"[116]—and the sooner we begin to be what we ought to be, the better off we are.

"Coming to Ourselves"

It is always a heartbreak to parents when children depart from right and respected ways, and it is always a hazard to youth—indeed to anyone—when they rebel against law, authority, or respectful consideration of counsels and precautions that could save much heartbreak and many mistakes.

We cannot avoid acute sorrow in seeing someone live so as to throw away his best chances for happiness and for high accomplishment in the living of his life. (The prodigal son is, of course, the case most cited of someone who first had to come to himself before he could properly appraise the things that forever mean the most.) But if only people could come to themselves sooner—for learning by living the wrong way is difficult and dangerous.

If youth could only better understand the position of parents! If parents could only help them better understand!

Surely it shouldn't be too difficult for youth to see that there is some value and advantage in the seasoning that parents have had, in judgment, in maturity; and that there are certainly some things that parents can save them. And yet somehow in every age we have before us the picture of parents praying and pleading, and earnestly seeking to save the next generation from making needless mistakes—earnestly trying to teach that happiness, and soundness, and safety and peace are found with respectful love of loved ones, and only within the respectful living of law.

The pleading of parents is not for narrow reasons—but only because of a great love and a great responsibility; only because they want their children to succeed, now and everlastingly in life; only because they want them to have happiness.

This is the only reason the Lord God Himself has given commandments, and the only reason parents pray and plead against youth's walking in careless or shortsighted ways.

And we would plead to those who have turned away from solid counsel, sound teaching, from waiting homes, and yearning hearts, to come to themselves, to turn back and not go one step farther down any wrong road.

Thank God for the power of repentance that somehow, sometime, touches and turns those who foolishly or carelessly have, for a time, followed wrong or wasteful ways.

When to Repent
and Improve...

We are disposed to attach particular significance to certain times and seasons. We look to special days and anniversaries and events. We speak of special hours—the eleventh hour, the midnight hour. We look to the clock and the calendar, and thus mark off the measures by which we live our lives.

Some hours and days and seasons have surely acquired special significance—and many things we seem to start or stop, or note, at some particular point—and these special times add their inducement to many things we do. All this is good—or may be—provided we don't let waiting for particular times lead us to delay repentance and improvement.

Well would we decide at any time, for the better, to do differently. We could decide at any moment, for example, to settle some difference, or to do some service; to begin to diet, if we need to; or to start to pay a debt past due; to begin to break a bad habit; to do better, to learn better, to live better, and not leave such decisions to a special day, to a special hour, to a particular time far future.

And if we pass a particular time for repenting

[157]

or improving, or if we falter or fail after having made a good resolution, we shouldn't postpone repentance or improvement for another special day or hour, or for another such season. It is important *now* to be repenting, *now* to be improving, *now* to be moving in the desired direction, not with needless dramatics but with a simple quiet consistency.

Life is everlasting, and the direction in which we move is exceedingly important, and the timing is also. And whether it's the New Year, or midnight, the eleventh hour or any other, there is no real reason for waiting for a special day, a special hour, or a special season to improve or to repent. When we need repentance, we need it *now*.

Not Beyond Our Reach...

We often think what we are going to do to-morrow, next week, next time, next season. We often plan; we often postpone. And sometimes, after postponing, we suddenly push ourselves at a fevered pace, and sometimes forget the effectiveness of quiet consistency.

With our human imperfections there will always be things we shall wish we had done differently, and always there are errors, and often we brood and blame ourselves for our failures. There are extremes in both directions: There are those who excuse and justify themselves too much, and those who blame themselves too much—and it isn't always easy to know where to draw the line between the two. A conscientious concern for whatever is less than it ought to be is an admirable and essential quality of character, but there is also such a thing as destroying effectiveness by magnifying mistakes.

There is no perfection in any of us, but one of the most sincerely satisfying assurances of life comes with the awareness that what the Lord God expects of us is not really beyond reach: respect and honesty and honor, consideration for others, faith and work, doing and enduring, the keeping of the commandments—and with these the future will unfold, if not with perfection, at least with an inner peace and purpose and a settled assurance.

Repentance is indeed the great principle of progress. Without it life would be less than hopeful, and lacking in incentive for us all. But with all our errors and failures, with all our regrets and wishing we had done differently, there is always this sustaining fact for our peace and for our ever lasting purpose: that the Lord God loves us and knows us and our needs—and that what He expects of us is not beyond our reach.

The Present Forever Faces
the Future

"The town clock is striking midnight. The cold of the night wind is urging its way in at the door and window-crevice; the fire has sunk almost to the third bar of the grate. Still my dream tires not, . . . Love has blended into reverence; passion has subsided into joyous content. And what if age comes, . . . What else gives inner strength, and knowledge, and a steady pilot-hand, to steer . . . out boldly upon that shoreless sea, where the river of life is running?"[117]

These *Reveries* written more than a century ago suggest a mood of much meaning. The river of life *is* running. And how short is the run into eternity! How swiftly the present becomes the past, as our lives are lived between memories and unknown events—as the present forever faces both past and future!

"If I were dying," said Justice Holmes, "my last words would be: have faith and pursue the unknown end. . . . There must be a drift, if one will go prepared and have patience, which will bring one out to daylight and a worthy end . . . one is safe in trusting to courage and to time."[118]

All this adds up to a kind of thoughtfulness, with some looking back but not too much brooding.

[161]

"Let us correct our errors forward, not backward."[115] The past is only good for what we have learned from it, the present for what we do with it, and the future is for faith—and the fact that we have come through all the past with the help of Providence, with a loving Father's mindfulness for us, is the best reason for faith in facing the future, with the love of family and of friends, with a humble wonder in the world, with repentance and a reappraisal of things that mean the most—and an awareness that there is an overruling Providence and Power, and a purpose which will prevail.

Thus may we "trust to courage and to time"— "have faith and pursue the unknown end."

Let the Years Unfold
with Faith

How often we wonder what undisclosed events are in the offing: Who of us will be here a year hence, and who will leave this life; who will see sorrow and who will see success? How often we wish we could see farther into the future, and how often we think that if we knew more we would do much better than we do.

But there are some things we *do* now know that we do not do. But often we ignore what we know. This is a subject which at another time we should like more fully to consider. But right now we should like to cite some profound and searching sentences from Emerson, which suggest that the Lord God will tell us what we need to know, will continue to reveal truth to us, or let us discover it for ourselves, as we are ready to receive it.

"God screens us evermore from premature ideas," he said. "Our eyes are holden that we cannot see things that stare us in the face, until the hour arrives when the mind is ripened, then we behold them, and the time when we saw them not, is like a dream."[119]

In another of his essays, Emerson offered this observation: "The popular notion of a revelation is, that it is a telling of fortunes . . . to tell from God how long men shall exist, what their hands shall do, and who shall be their company, . . . But we must pick no locks. We must check this low curiosity. . . . It is not in an arbitrary 'decree of God,' but in the nature of man that a veil shuts down on the facts of tomorrow; for the soul will not have us read any other but that of cause and effect."[120]

In short, as we sum up these sentences, it seems that we receive and understand and see about what we are ready and able and willing to receive and understand and see. And, as we are prepared for it, we shall not receive less of truth, less of understanding, than we are entitled to.

As we live the law, keep the commandments, use the hours and opportunities that are ours, as we acknowledge by our earnest actions what we *do* now know, then a loving, understanding Father will add all else we need to know. All things well and wisely used will be added unto, and all things earned will be ours. And with this quiet certainty of assurance we can let the years unfold with faith.

* * *

"Never forget the day of judgment. Keep it always in view. Frame every action and plan with reference to its unchanging decisions."[25]

—Carlyle

The Past, the Present...
and the Gift of Being
Grateful

"What do I owe to my times, to my country, to my neighbors, to my friends?— Such are the questions which a virtuous man ought often to ask himself."[121]
—John C. Lavater

"Causes" That Can Be
Counted On...

"Cause and effect, means and ends, seed and fruit, cannot be severed"; said Emerson, "for the effect already blooms in the cause, the end pre-exists in the means, the fruit in the seed. . . ."[36]

At the season when the harvest has been brought home we are earnestly thankful that the fruit *is* in the seed, that the harvest comes from causes that can be counted on, that the Creator is over all.

Of course, there are some who would say that we are indebted to chance, or that we live in a self-regulating universe. As to chance, Bruce Barton has given us this significant sentence: "When a load of bricks, dumped on a corner lot, can arrange themselves into a house; when a handful of springs and screws and wheels, emptied onto a desk, can gather themselves into a watch, then and not until then will it seem sensible, to some of us at least, to believe that all . . . [this] could have been created . . . all without any directing intelligence at all."[122]

Being altogether unconvinced that chance is the answer—being convinced that life did not create itself, or that law does not administer itself—what we now do, gratefully, is to give gratitude for all that God has given. We are thankful for the power to think, for the understanding that the glory of God is intelligence, for the privilege of life, for the conviction that its purpose is well worth all the effort, the improving, the repenting, the striving and the struggling and the daily doing of duty. We are thankful that such assurances carry us through difficult and discouraging days.

And with these lines, written some centuries since, we would say: ". . . humble yourselves . . . and worship God, in whatsoever place ye may be in, . . . and live in thanksgiving daily, for the many mercies and blessings which He doth bestow upon you,"[123] for ". . . if you should render all the thanks and praise which your whole soul has power to possess, to that God who has created you, and has kept and preserved you . . . and is preserving you from day to day, by lending you breath, that ye may live and move and do according to your own will, and even supporting you from one moment to another—I say, if ye should serve Him with all your whole souls yet ye would be unprofitable servants. And behold, all that He requires of you is to keep His commandments; . . ."[124] This heartfelt thanks we give for all that God has given.

Thanksgiving—the Fruits
of Faith

In its own way, the Thanksgiving season is the evidence of the fruition of faith. It is, in fact, "the substance of things hoped for"[125]—with the fruits of the field before us, the things that give us sustenance, the rich, bounteous blessings which are ours by the goodness of God, because someone had the faith to plow and to plant and because God gave the increase. So now we have our harvest.

And so much else we have also: life itself, for which each morning gratefully we should thank God as we wake to the wonder of a new day and know that there is yet a little time to do some things we should have done, time to move once more among the beloved, familiar places and people that we sometimes see with unseeing eyes— and sometimes take too much for granted.

When we see a photograph of something familiar we sometimes see something we haven't seen in the thing itself. Or when we see through the eyes of an artist—a painting, perhaps, of something we have come to consider as commonplace— we find that the artist has found for us something we couldn't see for ourselves. And at this thoughtful season we would well turn our eyes to see many cherished things as if we hadn't seen them—to

[169]

see, as if first seen, the goodness of all that God has given: life, our loved ones, food, work, and such surpassing blessings as freedom (which is not so common as some of us might have supposed), and the simple, wonderful, solid, sustaining things—with life to enjoy them, with loved ones and friends to share them, with freedom to use them, with grateful hearts to acknowledge them.

Yes, Thanksgiving is the evidence of faith, of the goodness of God, and of the blessing of willing work. God give us the good sense to step aside and see some things as if we had never really seen them—and give us the kind of gratitude that could never become bored with our blessings—and give us the grace to acknowledge humbly our dependence upon Providence, for "in nothing doth man offend God, or against none is his wrath kindled, save those who confess not his hand in all things. . . ."[126]

Among the greater qualities of character, among men and before God, is the great gift of gratitude.

On Taking Things
for Granted

There are times, perhaps, when all of us are moved by gratitude, and there are times when all of us may become careless about our blessings.

A favor done the first time is almost always appreciated. But a favor several times received may soon seem to be a commonplace occurrence and may even become a cause for complaint if it fails to be repeated as expected. Blessings which have been bestowed upon us often come to be looked upon as a continuing right.

So many things we may take for granted: health —until we lose it; food—until it is difficult to get; life—until it hangs in doubt—and many things besides. But it is not wise or well to take blessings or privileges for granted, however commonly they may occur: not the harvest of the year, nor our daily bread, nor the comfort of home, the love of those who wait there—nor freedom nor even life itself.

Nor must we expect to receive without giving, to prosper without working, to inherit without deserving.

And so, taking nothing for granted, we voice gratitude this day for all our blessings, naming only a few.

[171]

We are thankful that men may speak their minds; that public opinion and moral force are factors in fashioning our way of life, and that none are beyond their reach.

We are thankful for our many material blessings but more thankful for the measure of freedom that has survived in a world where much has not survived.

And with all that we are thankful for, we are aware that we must watch to see that things we are most thankful for shall not slip from us by the infiltration of false philosophies or by our own indifference to the dangers.

We are thankful for faith in the future—for faith that the future holds no problem too great to be surmounted by a thinking, working, repentant people.

For all our bounteous blessings we give gratitude to God, our Father, with fervent hope that we may never take them for granted. And in words from Shakespeare's Henry VI: "Let never day nor night unhallowed pass, but still remember what the Lord hath done."[127]

"A Land for Which Ye Did Not Labour"

In the history of ancient Israel there are some sobering sentences from Joshua for the solemn consideration of his people—and for us also: "And Joshua said unto all the people, Thus saith the Lord God of Israel . . . I brought your fathers out of Egypt . . . and the Egyptians pursued after your fathers with chariots and horsemen unto the Red sea. And when they cried unto the Lord, he put darkness between you and the Egyptians, and brought the sea upon them, and covered them; and your eyes have seen what I have done in Egypt . . . and I brought you into the land of the Amorites, . . . and they fought with you: and I gave them into your hand, . . . Then . . . the king of Moab, arose and warred against Israel, . . . And ye went over Jordan, and came unto Jericho: and the men of Jericho fought against you . . . and I delivered them into your hand . . .

And I have given you a land for which ye did not labour, and cities which ye built not, and ye dwell in them; of the vineyards and olive yards which ye planted not do ye eat. Now therefore fear the Lord, and serve him in sincerity and in truth."[128]

This is a sobering statment, not only anciently

[173]

but also unto us—for in a sense the Lord God has given unto us a land for which we did not labor. In a sense we have inherited liberty for which we did not labor.

We have a heritage of freedom and plenty and opportunity which seemingly no people of record ever before have had—and with so much handed us as a heritage it is sobering to suggest what might be expected of us in preserving and passing it on; and it is sobering to think what penalties might be imposed if indifferently we were to waste it away.

We aren't responsible for any history that reaches back before our own day. But we are responsible for what happens here and now so far as our influence and opportunities are concerned. And the Lord God who gave us what we have will not hold us guiltless if indifferently we fail to enter in to all that is expected of us—if indifferently we let the issues of the day be decided by default.

What Manner of Men
They Were....

Each generation runs its short run, leaving the future to take on some of the problems of the past, solving some and adding others, appraising principles, struggling with compromise, sometimes deviating, sometimes staying true to course. And as we see the stark reality of what our forebears faced, we wonder what ingredients of greatness went into the making of such men. If we could in reality realize what it would mean to enter an isolated area, with little more than a few simple tools—except for faith and freedom and courage and convictions and the willingness to work—we could then sense a little more what manner of men they were.

Nobody now seems much to move anywhere without many impedimenta, much paraphernalia, provision, costly equipment. But think of being far from a ready source of food, far from any source of supply—of being dependent upon the ability to gather and to get what the open country could provide. Think of being in the wilderness with no one to turn to—no one except themselves and divine Providence—and think of the extra closeness there would be to Him under such circumstances.

Much of what we have we would not have if our pioneer and pilgrim forebears had not laid their lives on the line. Everything we have that is worth having has come through the work and sacrifice of someone. And while conditions are not altogether comparable, the same principles still prevail, and we have to be willing to stand for something, to extend ourselves, willing to sacrifice, willing to work if we are to have and to hold that which matters most.

We cannot idle our way into affluence. We cannot keep even if we are digging deeper into debt. We cannot safely forget that the easy way is often harder than any other.

And we would plead with this generation not to ignore history, not to ignore principles, not to forget the price already paid—not to forget honor and honesty and the honoring of obligations; not to forget the willingness to prepare; not to forget sacrifice and service. If ever we draw more heavily upon the past than we replace, we shall be pursuing a course that is less than safe.

Thank God for the courage, for the faith, for the foresight, for the principles, the honor, the effort, and the downright devotion to duty of the pioneers and patriots of the past. And God grant that we may appreciate and preserve the heritage we have.

To All Our Ancestors...

Someone peering at a portrait of a great personality of the past was heard to say, altogether unimpressed: "Who's he? What did he do?"

We are often so absorbed in the present living of life, that we may be guilty of forgetting what we owe to people of the past. Each generation seems to acquire some sense of self-sufficiency, and to forget in part that others formerly occupied the places, and even perhaps the positions, that now are ours, and that through them we have the physical and mental and spiritual heritage we have.

True, the present generation, in a sense, owns and occupies the earth. Those who once held claim to it are no more with us. As for all that is tangible, they left it behind. A man lives his mortal life and moves on. "All the world's a stage," said Shakespeare.[129] The actors come and go. But in that brief time when they play their earthly part we are influenced by them more than now we know. What they were, what they did, has great effect on us.

No man stands alone in any generation, as to what he is or what he has. Nor is any generation sufficient unto itself, nor any person, ever. The past, plus what we are and what we do, helps to fashion the future. We are part of the procession of the whole human family. And a family album

[177]

or an ancient archive or the portraits of people, and what they were and what they did and what they learned and what they left, are all a very important part of the heritage we have.

To cite some scripture on the subject, "The heart of the fathers [shall turn] to the children, and the heart of the children to their fathers,"[130] —not only the fathers, but all forebears—for what they did and what they inseparably are to us is a matter of incalculable consequence. We are tied to them, and they to us through the succeeding years of time, into the endlessness of eternity. And the names and pictures of people of the past are sobering reminders of the fact that someone may soon be looking back and wondering who we were —and of the fact that there is an inseparable oneness of the whole human family.

* * *

". . . a man's ancestors have paid the price of what he is."[131]
                                            —Friedrich Nietzsche

Our Need of Others
—Always

"There is none so great but he may both need the help and service, . . . even of the meanest of mortals."[132]

—Seneca

Our Need of Others— Always

"The young, whether they know it or not," wrote Sir Richard Livingstone, "live on borrowed property."[133] All of us borrow much from many, from the present and the past, and we are deeply indebted to too many to mention. There are times in life when we may have feelings of self-sufficiency, times when things are well with us, when opportunities are open, and when we feel ourselves above the need we have of others. We may go through periods of satisfied self-assurance, and feel that it is not necessary either to consult or to consider others, and even interpret the interest of others in us as interference.

Children may sometimes feel this way about their parents, as well as about others, and be less gracious and feel less grateful, even to the point of supposing that they have outgrown others altogether, and are quite competent "to go it alone in life."

But there is no success that is permanently assured; there is no assurance against sorrow; there is no one who may not at some time know loss and loneliness; there is no one who may not sometime know real need. We all have great need of each other—or at least we cannot know that we shall not have need.

No man alone is ever altogether adequate, altogether safe, or altogether assured that he may not have need of someone—soon. There is wisdom in counsel; there is safety in good company; there is something good about keeping close to family and good friends.

And to young people particularly, and to all others also, we would plead always to keep the spirit of consideration, the spirit of respect, gratitude, humility, with an awareness that there is wisdom beyond our own small wisdom, and strength beyond our own small self-assurance. There is wisdom in keeping close to loved ones, and to the Lord God, and the keeping of his commandments.

We all need others, always, whether we know it or not, and we may none of us ever safely assume that we have surely arrived, or that we are quite prepared "to go it alone in life."

Impersonal People

In the normal course of living there are many pleasantries that pass from person to person. There is also much social veneer and much perfunctory impersonal politeness.

For example, we may more or less automatically ask others how they are, often not waiting for an answer or really expecting one. Often two people in passing ask the question at the same time, with neither one waiting for an answer from the other. This practice comes perhaps from complex living among many people under conditions of pressure and preoccupation. Such salutations, though somewhat superficial, may serve their useful purpose. But if a person really wants someone to tell his troubles to, the chances are he will have a difficult time finding an open ear among the usual run of those who ask without slowing their pace to hear the reply.

Somewhere along the way in life we must reach down deeper and discover the substance beneath the surface—for if our concern, our inquiry of others is habitually impersonal—if those we pass in public places, those whom we serve in our various capacities, are to us merely impersonal people, merely population, we shall find that we have only shallow understanding of others and shall see little below the surface.

All men have their troubles, their problems, whether we know of them or not. All have their hopes and heartaches, their need of others, their feelings of frustration. All need someone to talk to, someone to counsel with. All men need understanding. And all men have some claims upon us—the claim of having a common Father, the claim of being fellow occupants of the same earth. And He who marks the sparrow's fall—and He who walked among men, and blessed the children and healed the sick and showed His concern for each one—surely He would expect more from all of us for all of us than some of our thoughtless and impersonal practices would suggest.

People—in a Personal Way

We are sometimes disposed to look upon people and their problems impersonally. In a world of so many millions of men, other people —that is other than ourselves—tend to become population per square mile, prospects for our products, customers for our shoes or our shirts, clients for our services, votes for our political parties, patrons for our performances.

But we can't separate a man from himself, and we can't override the fact that each man inherently has rights and hopes and a heart and a personal potential and possibilities. There is no such thing as an impersonal person, and one of the things we can least afford to lose in our modern manner is a personal attitude toward people. The mass must not let us lose sight of the individual man. Bigness must not let us lose sight of human qualities and character. Numbers must not replace names. Statistics must not take from us a sincere individual interest in others.

These passengers who push their way with us on public conveyances; these drivers who impatiently honk horns in traffic tangles; these who crowd to the counter, who buy things, who need things, who want things; these millions who live in the millions of homes the inside of which we never see; these who crowd the classrooms, the hospitals, the public places; and these others whom we read about remotely—all are people in a very personal way, people with hopes and heartaches and sorrows and successes.

All are eternal, individual, important personalities; all are children of the Father who is the Father of us all, who gave us life, who has plans and purposes for each of us, who has set before us the opportunities of our existence for endless progress and possibilities. The child, the boy and the girl, the mother, the mature and able man, the aged and the infirm—each one is a person; and the sooner all of us know that everyone else is a personal person (and the sooner we act as if we knew it), the sooner we shall have a foretaste of a heaven on earth.

The Basis of Credit
and Confidence...

Sometimes when feelings of self-sufficiency seem to assert themselves, when people feel sure that they no longer have need of others, we need to remind ourselves that no man can be sure he will not have need of others, ever, nor be sure that he will not need someone soon, no matter how successful or how assured life looks.

In pursuing this theme we must come to an inevitable conclusion, indeed to one of the foremost lessons of life: that the quality of humility is one of the great qualities of character, and there is no real greatness in anyone without it.

And now to follow back the thread by which we come to this conclusion: Sometimes when men lose the quality of humility, when they become cocksure, they may feel that they are above the rules and principles that apply to others. And in this misconception they may cast off friends, cast off obligations, cast off principles and conventions, and use all circumstances to suit themselves, even as an opportunist. But the opportunist is always in a precarious position—and may indeed cast off many things, the need of which he knows not until perhaps he knows the need a little too late—for the time to make friends is all along the way of life;

the time to build credit is before we are urgently in need of credit; the time to become acquainted with the Lord God is before the pressure of necessity is upon us.

We ought to establish the basis of confidence, of credit, of trust, with our friends, our family, with all men, and with the Lord God before we find ourselves in too deep a deficit—before we find ourselves at an inconvenient time, and under urgent necessity seeking for the credit, the favors, the friendship, the blessings, and understanding that we shall surely sometime need.

Our Debt to Those We Never Knew...

Life, as we live it, is made possible by the services of many people. Whether we think so or not, we are none of us self-made, self-sustaining, or self-sufficient. We are dependent upon all the Lord God gives and has given, and we are dependent upon innumerable things that other people do and have done, that other people learn and have learned, that other people make and have made—and the great ideal of work, of service, of doing for others, of co-operative effort, is what keeps us alive, with enrichment of life.

We are indebted to others not only for knowledge and things and services, but even for companionship itself. And in the plans and purposes of God there is an endless service and society, including a cherished circle of family and friends upon whom we are dependent for completeness. No man is sufficient unto himself. We owe an obligation to forebears along a long line, and to others yet to come in a long and endless line.

All of us have reason to be interested in all of us, with obligations to the past and to the far future—with an obligation to help keep free those who follow, and to pass to them as good or better what we ourselves have received.

All of us have reason to be helpful and to have understanding hearts, for we are dependent upon more people, past and present, than we have any real awareness of, and are more dependent upon Divine Providence than we have any real awareness of—with obligations to work, to serve, to cherish, to understand, forgive, help, encourage. We all of us owe much to innumerable others, many of whom we never knew—and to ancestors, who, in this life, we never saw—and gratitude to God for all that He has given.

"And he shall turn the heart of the fathers to the children, and the heart of the children to their fathers. . . ."[130] Not in any real sense is any man without obligation to others—past, or present, or yet far future.

The Moving Power of Prayer

There likely isn't a much greater loneliness than the loneliness of a man who cannot find comfort and assurance and help outside himself. And there likely isn't much greater loneliness than the loneliness of a man who has never found effectively in his life the great and moving power of prayer.

Prayer is an incalculable source of strength, of peace, of courage, of comfort—the comfort that comes with knowing that there is a Source of help, wisdom, guidance, outside ourselves, outside of human sources. Men seem to rise to greatness when most sincerely humble, and never more sincerely humble do they seem than when approaching their Father in prayer, in acknowledging the debts, the favors, the blessings of past and present. We are moved by the thought of patriots in prayer, and by the prayerful approach to public problems.

It is proper to pray for all men, even our enemies. It is proper to pray that the spirit of peace may move the hearts even of those who intend no peace, to pray that their ill intent may somehow be softened.

Some of the most sublime moments of life are the moments when prayers are remembered: the prayer of a child at a mother's knee, or the prayer of loved ones waiting; the prayer in time of illness, of sorrow, and in the problems and decisions of each day—the prayer of gratitude to God.

It would be presumptuous to say that we understand the process of prayer, the means by which a man, in his need, can send his spoken or unspoken thoughts or the burden of his most sincere desires to a Source whence cometh help. But the unseen forces that we are already aware of should give us faith in other unseen forces.

"We don't know the millionth part of 1 per cent about anything," said Thomas A. Edison. "We don't know what water is. We don't know what electricity is. We don't know what heat is. We have a lot of hypotheses about these things, but that is all. But we do not let our ignorance about these things deprive us of their use."[134] Nor should we let our lack of knowledge concerning the means and channels through which prayer moves deprive us of its use. Considering all the unseen forces there are, it is but a short step of faith to accept the fact that our Father in his infinite wisdom can and does know the needs of us all, our attitudes, our pleas and petitions, the crying out of the human heart, and does not leave those pleas unheard or unheeded.

* * *

"God has made no one absolute. . . . No one subsists by himself alone."[135]
—Owen Feltham

Our Lord, Our Loved Ones—and Everlasting Life

We are born for a higher destiny than that of earth."[136]

—Edward G. Bulwer-Lytton

The Word of Witnesses

In law we confirm a past occurrence with the word of witnesses. In scripture it is recorded "that in the mouths of two or three witnesses every word may be established."[137] History as it is recorded and read is also largely the word of witnesses. We ourselves did not see the sights and scenes or the people of the past, or the deeds that other men did. We accept much on the word of witnesses.

With this in mind we turn to events concerning Jesus of Nazareth, the Master of mankind, who was born of Mary in Bethlehem; whose birth was marked by unusual events; who, at the age of twelve, reasoned with the learned in the temple; who, while yet a young man, emerged to perform the mission that His Father, the Lord God, had given Him; who walked the shores of Galilee, who chose His apostles from humble, teachable men; who went down into the water with John to be baptized in the River Jordan; who was tempted of Satan; who healed the sick and comforted the sorrowing and called to repentance the sinners; who blessed the children, stilled the tempest, and walked upon the waters; who fed the multitudes; who made the blind to see and the dead to rise; who gathered many followers; was falsely accused, betrayed by one of his own, taken by armed guards

[195]

in the Garden; tried, denied, condemned to death; cruelly nailed upon the cross, and died and was tenderly laid in a borrowed tomb, guarded by soldiers; and who rose and came forth from death to life on the third day, and appeared unto friends and loved ones, and a multitude of men, and was taken unto the Lord God in Glory, to take His place by His Father's side, as Paul said, and as Stephen saw, and as others also saw.

All this is recorded, all this is witnessed by the word of many witnesses, and witnessed by the more sure witness of the Spirit that speaks to our very souls; and by the transforming power of the Gospel that changes the lives of men and gives them peace and purpose.

"And now, after the many testomonies which have been given of Him, this is the testimony, last of all, which we give of Him: that He lives!"[138] "I know that my Redeemer liveth."[139] Whatever else may have been added unto it, this, essentially, is the meaning of Christmas: that Jesus is the Christ, our Lord and Savior, the Messiah—as witnessed by the word of many witnesses.

Home—and Christmas

What can one say for a season where so much is intermixed? There is thoughtfulness for others, but a thoughtfulness preoccupied with a bustling of busy-ness. Nor could one deny that sentiment is encouraged partly by commercial motive—but the sentiment is there, a sentiment set apart from all other times and seasons, with many buying for others, few for themselves.

Whether or not all this is always wise, whether or not there are some excesses, whether or not it is partly compulsion, the compulsion of expectancy, of custom, the compulsion of comparisons, is something which by itself should sometime be considered—nevertheless, not at any other time are hearts so intent on doing so much for so many, moved by a spirit which is real, and different, and which runs down deep, despite all the mixture of motives. And there is kindliness—a kindliness that comes of Him who "so loved the world, that he gave his only begotten Son,"[140]—a love that refines the heart, that turns thoughts homeward, that makes absent ones more missed and those present much more precious, and moves men to do something for someone besides themselves.

As to the homeward turning: ". . . I pity him whose soul does not leap at the mere utterance of that name [of home] . . . ," wrote Donald Grant

Mitchell. "It is not the house, though that may have its charms; nor the fields . . . streaked with your own footpaths;—nor the trees, though their shadow be to you like that of a great rock in a weary land;—nor yet is it the fireside; . . . nor the pictures which tell of loved ones, nor the cherished books,—but more far than all these—it is the Presence. The Lares of your worship are there; the altar of your confidence there; the end of your worldly faith is there; and adorning it all, . . . is the ecstasy of the conviction, that there at least you are beloved; that there you are understood; that there your errors will meet ever with gentlest forgiveness; . . . that there you may unburden your soul, fearless of harsh, unsympathizing ears; and that there you may be entirely and joyfully—yourself!"[117]

Thus all things turn home at this season of blessedness, of kindliness, of a love that comes from a Father who sent His Son that we might have life and loved ones everlastingly—which is His greatest gift.

For "God Saw That It Was Good"

In commenting on Christmas, may we pass for a moment the usual texts that we might turn to, and take one from far back, from the first book of the Bible, that recalls how the Creator of heaven and earth looked over what had been brought into being—"and God saw that it was good."[141]

And it *was* good: a beautiful and bounteous earth with its seasons and its sustenance, with forests and fields, the sun and the sea, the fruits and flowers, the meadows and mountains, and so much else unmentioned given for our good by a loving Father in whose image men were made.

The centuries and the ages have come and gone since then. The earth has seen its sorrows, its setbacks, its peace, and its progress. The prophets have often been stoned in their own ages and accepted in others. The world has seen dark days and dark deeds—but under and over all has been an always-emerging truth that could never be permanently suppressed in the unfolding of the plans and purposes of Providence.

And despite the mistakes that men have made, despite discouraging circumstances and situations, the cruel contrasts, ignorance, and adversity, despite it all, there is so much that is good within

[199]

the limits of this life, and so much reason for faith in the future. The spirit of Christmas is in itself one of the evidences of a finer future that gives a glimpse of hope, almost, it seems, a glimpse of heaven.

As Christmas comes, let it be a time that lights the eyes of children and puts laughter on their lips. Let it be a time for lifting the lives of those who live in loneliness; let it be a time for calling our families together, for feeling a nearness to those who are near to us, and a nearness also to those who are absent. Let it be a time of prayers for peace, for the preservation of free principles, and for the protection of those who are far from us. Let it be a time for re-examining ourselves, and for dedicating our lives to the values that endure.

As Christmas comes let it be a new witness to the world of the mission and message of Jesus the Christ, the Son of God, our Saviour, the Prince of Peace. Let it be a time for thanksgiving, for faith in a finer future that ever comes closer as each Christmas comes—for "God saw that it was good" —and it was and is and will be good in the eternal working out of His plans and purposes.

"This Same Jesus..."

Of such a day as this, a Scottish poet wrote: "The holy spirit of the Spring is working silently."[142] And Tennyson added: "Once more the Heavenly Power makes all things new, . . ."[143]

Goethe said it in these sentences, "So then the year is repeating its old story again. We are come once more, thank God! to its most charming chapter. The violets and the . . . flowers are as its inscriptions or vignettes. It always makes a pleasant impression on us, when we open again at these pages of the book of life."[144]

Opening again at the pages of the book of life is, this day, a theme of exceeding significance since, some nineteen centuries ago, Jesus the Christ walked among men and proclaimed the eternal precepts of life everlasting. His coming was foretold by prophets whose words are witnessed in the written record. His ministry, His message, His miracles, were witnessed by a multitude of men— as also was the reality of His resurrection, as He appeared to his apostles and to many others also, "being seen of them forty days, and speaking of the things pertaining to the kingdom of God: . . . And when he had spoken these things, while they beheld, he was taken up; and a cloud received him out of their sight. And while they looked stedfastly toward heaven as he went up, behold, two men stood by them in white apparel; Which also said, Ye men of Galilee, why stand ye gazing up into heaven? this same Jesus, which is taken up from you into heaven, shall so come in like manner as ye have seen him go into heaven."[145]

His divinity, the literal reality of His resurrection, and His coming again on earth is the very foundation of Christian faith, and the assurance unto all men of everlasting life. And this day we would witness of the certainty of such assurance—the assurance that personality is perpetuated, and truth and intelligence, and that, for all of us, everlasting life with our loved ones is the very essence and intent of heaven and the hereafter—the prime motive of our Father's plan and purpose.

"The holy spirit of the Spring is working silently." "We open again at these pages of the book of life." "Once more the Heavenly Power makes all things new, . . ."

"O Man, Whosoever Thou Art..."

There is a long-told tale of Alexander the Great, who paused, at the age of thirty-two at the tomb of Cyrus the Great—Cyrus who had preceded Alexander by some two centuries. Each in his own time had conquered virtually all he could see, and had acquired more than his understanding could encompass. And Alexander, at the tomb of Cyrus, pondered this inscription:

"O man, whosoever thou art, and from whence-soever thou comest (for I know thou wilt come), I am Cyrus, the founder of the Persian empire; do not grudge me this little earth which covers my body."[146] And it is said that Alexander, who died soon thereafter, was sobered by the shortness of the glory that once was.

We would make no apology for enjoying and appreciating, and even in a measure pursuing the material gifts of life: comforts and conveniences, good food, a solid house and home; the beauty of the earth, the richness of its soil and its resources —all this that God has given. All this, if we read rightly, the Lord God intended his children to have and to enjoy, "with prudence and thanksgiving" —provided there is also balance and the good sense to pursue also truth and intelligence and the mental and spiritual intangibles.

The material part of creation is surely an important part in the Creator's purpose. But however much a man can hold in his hands, there seems to be no limit to what he can hold in his heart—no limit to the satisfaction of service; and no price that he can put on good character, good mind, broad understanding; the love of loved ones and the love of learning; appreciation for people; the beauty of a sunset or of the autumn air; the peace and blessing of a quiet conscience; or the wonderful awareness of being alive, or the assurance of some everlasting certainties.

The Lord God gave man dominion over all the earth, and the quest for things seems proper and appropriate—good things—and the making of good things much more—so long as possessions are not permitted to possess him. But beyond all this—surpassing all this—is the assurance a man may have within his soul: the assurance that truth and intelligence, and he himself, and loved ones and the love of loved ones, extend beyond time into the endlessness of eternity.

Loved Ones Gone... and Loved Ones Living...

"Each departed friend," wrote one eminent observer, "is a magnet that attracts us to the next world."[147]

It is true that our interest becomes divided, as those we love leave us. Some things hold us here, and some things pull us away. And always and ever we live with memories, with remembrance—always with some of the same questions, the same searching for assurance of the everlastingness of life.

There is this to be said, aside from all other assurances: that no loving Father would plan, in his providence, that we should learn so much of life and learn so much to love only to let us lose both life and those whom most we love. Life is its own evidence of plan and purpose. And everlasting life is no more a miracle, no less possible, no less real than this life we live.

And to those who mourn and those who remember, we would reaffirm the faith, indeed the solid assurance, that personality and truth and intelligence are perpetuated, and that memories are not only for the past, not only for the present, but also for the future—not only for what was, but also for what will yet be. All reason supports the everlastingness of life, as well as the assurance that God has given.

And now may we turn for a moment from memories and remembrance to a present look at life: Besides remembering memories, may we, please God, come closer to those who are with us yet. The line of life, the line between time and eternity, is a thin line of no certain length. And may we remember to be more thoughtful of family and friends; to be more with them; more mindful of them, more courteous, more kind, more willing to make, now, more wonderful memories for the future—and more enjoy, more appreciate loved ones living, that we may have more to tie us to life now, and more faith for the future, and more memories to sustain us in any short separation.

"Each departed friend is a magnet that attracts us to the next world," and may each loved one living tie us to this life we live, and to loved ones everlastingly.

* * *

". . . I know that my redeemer liveth . . ."
—Job 19:25

A Look at What We Do With Life...

"Much may be done in those little shreds and patches of time, which every day produces, and which most men throw away . . ."[72]

—Caleb C. Colton

What Takes Our Time...?

To quote Carlyle: "Men do less than they ought, unless they do all that they can."[25]

In this day and season of many pressures, we frequently feel we ought to do more than we reasonably can. We feel both the shortness of time and the magnitude of our tasks. We think of knowledge we wish we had acquired, of talents we wish we had improved, of service we wish we had given, of things we wish were ready, of work we wish we had behind us—and no matter how much we do each day, we frequently feel ourselves frustrated, and frequently spread ourselves so thin that we fail to be fully effective.

We intend so much, but get caught in the mechanics of living, in the routine, in the daily detail, some of which is exceedingly essential and some of which is much less so. But no matter how much we do or fail to do, we must sometime arrive at an awareness that we will always have to choose what we will permit to take our time. This is a matter of daily, of hourly, decision: what is most important, what to give first place—and what should be secondary.

On this point James Bryce had this to say a half century or so ago: "If thoroughness is a virtue to be cultivated, still more is time a thing to be saved. The old maxim, 'Whatever is worth doing is worth doing well,' is less true than it seems, and has led many people into a lamentable waste of time. Many things are worth doing if you can do them passably well with a little time and effort, which are not worth doing thoroughly if so to do them requires much time and effort. Time is the measure of everything in life, and every kind of work ought to be adjusted to it. One of the commonest mistakes we all make is spending ourselves on things whose value is below the value of the time they require. . . ."[148]

It isn't the feverish pace nor the sudden impulse that is most effective, nor the boastful biting off of what is too big. It is the steady purpose, the quiet conscience, the doing of duty, the finishing, the enduring, the seeing things through, the thoughtful quiet consistency—always with an awareness that among life's most important decisions is what we permit to take our time—"for which," said William Penn, "God will certainly reckon . . . with us, when Time shall be no more."[54]

"May I Have a Minute of Your Time?"

History is long. The great sweep of time and eternity is long—endlessly long—but the mortal life of each of us is not. And whether we live short lives, or long, the years move swiftly—from the freer years of youth, through the period of preparation, to a period of performance—then on to the real and glorious opportunities of eternity.

And no matter how old the aged seem to youth, and no matter how young the young seem to those who are old, the young and the old are not so far apart, and "one event happeneth to them all."[149]

And now a moment about the man who says "May I have a minute of your time?" Usually, he doesn't really mean a minute, and the minute he asks for is often multiplied.

We could give him money—and maybe make more. We could give him goods—and manufacture more. But as to time—it "is the [very] stuff life is made of,"[150] and in a very real sense we are responsible for the time we take from our own lives and from others.

And when we ask a man for a moment—or much more—do we take his time for trivia, or do we add meaning and understanding to his life?

Would we take his time for what would tempt him, for what would burden or enslave him, for what would fill his heart with regret, or his mind with unpleasant memories? Or for what would build him up, and add to health and happiness and peace and progress?

In a very real sense we are responsible for what we take time for, our own and that of others. In a very real sense we are responsible for the ideas and impressions we let loose.

For this reason we are deeply aware of the sacred trust and responsibility of entering other men's hearts and homes and lives by any means whatsoever, for all of us have a responsibility for the time we take, for the influence we have, for our total effect on others.

Tied with Red Tape...

Having in mind those who say, "If I do this for you, I'll have to do it for everyone," we here cite the parable of the Good Samaritan as to serving someone when the need is now, as to doing something when a person with a real problem presents himself—even when it is after hours. With this in mind let us turn to what is called red tape—by which we mean, essentially, getting lost in procedures, procedures which may be altogether arbitrary, which may be quite apart from principles, and which are sometimes made to seem even more important than people or than solving problems.

"More than one splendid idea," said a significant source, "has been launched to accomplish a great good only to wind up as an institution more interested in maintaining its routine of procedure rather than in spreading its splendid idea."[151]

Procedures, like habits, are likely to take hold, even when they emphasize the form rather than the basic facts. Order is surely essential—and surely also are certain procedures—but when we become too tightly tied up in red tape, common sense and effectiveness and efficiency may cease to function, with arbitrary waste of time, unnecessary delays, making people stand around in needless long lines.

[213]

The Master once said something about an ox in the pit—which we take to mean doing something about something when the need is now.

What is called red tape is sometimes essential. Technicalities are sometimes essential. There are requirements; there are procedures; there are principles that cannot—must not—be set aside. But sometimes red tape is simply a procedure that somehow got started and that no one has taken the trouble to stop.

Whenever needlessly we take people's time, or insist on meaningless motions, or make men wait in long lines, or insist on unessential procedures we are wasting irreplaceable time and effort and energy. We should never needlessly waste men's lives in waiting rooms or in long lines, and never needlessly tie their hands with red tape.

Fretfulness … and Thoughtfulness

F rom Mendelssohn's *Elijah,* we would take a scriptural text, with words that run along these lines: "The harvest now is over, the summer days are gone."[152] There are times when all of us become acutely aware of the swift passing of the seasons, and of the days and hours as they seem exceedingly short.

When we are so absorbed in daily details, it is sometimes difficult to keep a sense of direction. "To know where you are is a good thing," said a sentence recently read: But "It is as important and perhaps more so, to know where you are going."[153] But this also we would add: It is also a good thing to know why.

There has to be purpose to make things meaningful. The idle and aimless motions, time-passing without a sense of purpose, give a listlessness to life. And if we had a word to suggest today it would be "thoughtfulness"—thoughtfulness in pausing to consider the point and purpose of all we do.

A sentence from Thomas Hood suggests an attitude at least occasionally becoming: "Stand shadowless," he said, "like silence, listening to silence."[154]—listening, thinking, a little away from the rush and the routine—a little time taken for

[215]

the quieting of the spirit, for the slowing of the pulse, for reflection, for some serenity; a little freedom from the fevered pace, a little time for appraising the purpose.

We often wonder. We often worry. We some-times spend some sleepless hours. We turn things over in our minds with wearying anxiety. But *fretfulness* is no substitute for *thoughtfulness*— the thoughtfulness that quiets the spirit, that ponders, that prays, that thoughtfully appraises, and that doesn't let itself get lost in routine, in the trivia of daily detail. Life is a search, and the purpose of the search should not be lost sight of in the swiftly passing seasons.

And we would plead for the slowing of the pace that moves too fast to absorb the meaning of the passing scenes. We would plead for prayerful pausing, for thoughtfulness, for more awareness of the ultimate aim, before the harvest is over, before the summer days are gone.

"A Short Walk...that Never Ends"

"Life is a short walk along a narrow thread ... beginning and ending in a mysterious unknown. Hope keeps us balanced as we walk the narrow line. Life is short as we see it, but in reality . . . never ends—and, long or short, it is all that we have."[155]

Life *is* all we have. There are times when we would like to keep it as it is, freeze it, in a sense; keep it from changing—times when we have our families and friends around us, when we have enjoyed some success, when we are in health and happiness. There are lovely days and lovely hours which we dislike leaving behind, but we are ever more aware that we cannot hold on to any hour.

Sometimes we have regrets, and wonder what would have happened if we had done differently —but we can't go back. We must always move ahead—always with some problems, with some unanswered questions, with some uncertainties, with some seeming injustices. We often feel we would like to see the future, and often feel we would like to change the past. There are some experiences we would like to eliminate from life, and some we would like again to live—to re-run part of the picture.

But as to the whole picture, we are in no position to appraise it. We see only a short segment, and must learn to live with the faith and solid assurance that the record and accounts are being kept, that the books will be balanced, that all will receive all they are entitled to, and that no one will be unjustly dealt with in the eternities that follow time.

Life is all we have—a life of endless length; and there is great purpose and meaning and reason for living, and reason for learning, for trying, for trusting, for improving, for repenting, with a great gratitude for family and friends, with a great appreciation of the importance of principles, and great compassion for people and their problems.

The Closing of the Calendar

So soon the cycle has once more swiftly turned itself, and suddenly we have come again to the closing of the calendar. It seems only a few short weeks since we were watching another calendar close, since we were watching another winter, another spring, watching another growing season. Only a few short days, it seems, since summer. And as we face this breathless flight of future days there is a sobering thoughtfulness in realizing that the years are running rapidly—a sobering thoughtfulness that suggests we pause to look at what we do with life.

Actually there is no alchemy in the closing of the calendar. Actually the curtain opens next day on about the same scene. The nature of man doesn't change much over night, and we are not likely to wake up on any morning greatly different from what we were. (Change, for the better at least, is likely to come with quiet resolution and quiet consistency.) But we may well wake up wondering whether we have made the most of the closing period of the past; wondering what we could have done differently; what we might have done that we didn't do.

This is a time, too, that suggests settlement. The blessed relief of paying a debt is surpassingly satisfying, even as the burden of an unpaid debt is doggedly discouraging. With an unsatisfied obligation we don't quite own ourselves. We don't quite own our talents or our time. There is always a claim and encumbrance upon the future when a debt is coming due. But the man who learns to live within his means finds the future ever easier to face.

In addition to debts in matters of money, there are other obligations also: debts of gratitude; debts to parents, to loved ones; debts to others for service received—debts for sweet service for which there is no entry on the books. There is the debt of doing our part in life, the debt to Him who gave us the privilege and blessing of life. All these debts are as real as those that are kept in formal accounts.

And there are differences to be settled, as well as debts. If there are those whom we cannot face with good feeling, if there are those near us with whom we cannot feel free because of some unhappy act or utterance, the closing calendar suggests that we do what can and should be done to dissolve unsettled differences.

The sands are running; the hands are turning as time moves on to eternity, and no day, no year, should come to its close without the settling of debts and differences to the best of our ability.

* * *

"And the time that remains is time enough, if we will only stop the waste and the idle, useless regretting."[156]
—Arthur Brisbane

"Book of Beginnings, Story Without End..."

"What then? Shall we sit idly down and say
The night hath come; it is no longer day?
The night hath not yet come; we are not quite
Cut off from labor by the failing light;
Something remains for us to do or dare;
Even the oldest tree some fruit may bear; . . ."[157]

—Henry Wadsworth Longfellow

"Book of Beginning, Story Without End..."

"How beautiful is youth! how bright it gleams
With its illusions, aspirations, dreams!
Book of Beginnings, Story without End,
Each maid a heroine, and each man a friend!"[157]

Longfellow leaves these lines on the bright look of youth and turns to some lines on the later years of life:

"By Time, the great transcriber, on his shelves,
Wherein are written the histories of ourselves.
What tragedies, what comedies, are there;
What joy and grief, what rapture and despair!
What chronicles of triumph and defeat,
Of struggle, and temptation, and retreat!
What records of regrets, and doubts, and fears!
What pages blotted, blistered by our tears!"[157]

There are many things that come between the early and the later years of life: hopes, desires; some triumphs, some success; some happy moments we would keep forever—some moments we would wish were never there; some problems, some sorrows; some disappointment in ourselves, some in others; sometimes the crying out for answers; sometimes a little losing of the way—with the wish to see a little farther into the future—some search-ing, groping, wondering, longing, with the need to know the purpose, with the need for the assur-ance of some certainties.

Such assurance, blessedly, God has given, with some awareness of His purpose implanted within, some still small voice of conscience, some intima-tions of the answers, some lighting of the way in our choosing, our deciding, in our doing and en-during—with a Father who would welcome us as we improve, repent; as earnestly we endeavor to be worthy of that welcome.

"But why, you ask me, should this tale be told To men grown old, or who are growing old? It is too late! Ah, nothing is too late Till the tired heart shall cease to palpitate. . . . The unwritten only still belongs to thee: Take heed, and ponder well what that shall be."[157]

The Challenge of Aging...

"Whatever poet, orator, or sage
May say of it, old age is still old age.
It is the waning, not the crescent moon;
The dusk of evening, not the blaze of noon:
It is not strength, but weakness; not desire,
But its surcease; not the fierce heat of fire,
The burning and consuming element,
But that of ashes and of embers spent,
In which some living sparks we still discern,
Enough to warm, but not enough to burn.

What then? Shall we sit idly down and say
The night hath come; it is no longer day?
The night hath not yet come; we are not quite
Cut off from labor by the failing light;
Something remains for us to do or dare;
Even the oldest tree some fruit may bear;
                    *   *   *
For age is opportunity no less
Than youth itself, though in another dress."[157]

The growing ever older is the only way of living life, and the possibilities of age are impellingly important. ". . . the arms best adapted to old age are culture and the active exercise of virtues." ". . . so far from being listless and sluggish, old age . . . [should be] even a busy time, always doing and attempting something, with active exercise . . . and temperance . . ."[53] The fact is, each part of life has its own advantages and disadvantages. Each has its qualities and conditions to be met and to be adjusted to, and in the lengthening years of life one should keep active, useful, and always in pursuit of some impelling interest, some good purpose, something that serves the present and looks to the future, without fear of passing days or of lengthening shadows, but with gratitude for what has been, for what is yet to be, and for the blessed assurance God has given that truth and intelligence and life and loved ones and purpose and personality are everlasting. And ". . . for . . . one [who] is so old as to think that he may not live a year. . . . [let him plant] his trees to serve a race to come, . . ."[53]

Some Attitudes and Opportunities of Age

Among the most wasteful of all the wastes of the world is the waste of time, of thought, of human effort and energy, of talents and creative gifts and productive powers. The world needs more of most good things than all men can make, both of substance and of services. Its real needs are never really satisfied. Not all the children are ever taught. Not all the sick are ever cared for. Not all the unfortunate and needy are ever included in adequate opportunities.

Not all those in confusion or in sorrow are ever fully counseled and comforted. Furthermore there is always room for more of everything uplifting —great literature, art, music, beauty of the living, creative, wholesome kind. And for anyone arbitrarily to cut off his period of productivity is a waste, a loss, that cannot be calculated, but for which somehow, somewhere there must surely be an accounting. Indeed He who gave us life has not, that we know of, established any point at which we should cease well to use our time and talents.

Now with this as a preface, may we cite some lines from several sources: George Bernard Shaw said: "I want to be thoroughly used before I die, and I want to die gloriously solvent, intellectually, morally, and financially."[158] ". . . Initiative and effort must be made . . . to maintain . . . health."[159] ". . . Let each man proportion his efforts to his powers."[53] "Whilst I yet live," said Addison, "let me not live in vain."[160] There is no wealth but life,"[161] said John Ruskin. And since this is so, it would not be well to waste it at any age.

But men need to know that they are needed—that they have some responsibility, that someone is counting on them, that there is something essential or significant that demands their getting up and getting going—that demands their exerting themselves, that demands the meaningful use of time and effort and energy. Any or all of us would likely let down without some challenging activity, without some significant assignment, and always we ought somehow to be able to organize ourselves to use our God-given powers—at whatever age. "Life is not a goblet to be drained; it is measure to be filled."[162]

Lengthening the Productive Period...

When we talk of the attitudes and opportunities of age, we are talking also to youth—for the years move swiftly from the younger to the later years of life—and it is, as Cicero said: ". . . the honorable conduct of [youth] . . . that is rewarded by possessing influence at the last . . . If one has lived . . . well . . . the harvest . . . is wonderful."[53]

And now to look a moment at the brief span that could be called the productive period: A lot of life is used in getting started, and in the complexities of modern living it doesn't seem probable that the period of preparation would soon be shortened. Indeed, we may look to its lengthening.

Since this is so, there comes a question as to whether or why ye should shorten the period of productivity? When it takes so long to get started, should we discourage people from using their gifts and powers as long as possible? We could cite many examples of men who have lived long and have produced remarkably in the lengthening years of life; and since there are so many, we would suppose that there could be many, many more, and that it is partly a matter of attitude and opportunity. "Use what you have," said Cicero, "and

[229]

whatever you may chance to be doing, do it with all your might. . . . [with your] mind at full stretch like a bow, and never [give] in to . . . age by growing slack. . . . For myself, I had rather be an old man a somewhat shorter time than an old man *before* my time."[53]

Contrast this with what Hugo Grotius, in his last words, unhappily said of himself: "I have spent my life laboriously doing nothing."[163]

"Life," said Carlyle, "is not given us for the mere sake of living. . . ."[164]

All this, in summary, seems essentially to suggest: that there is urgent need for all the good things that all of us can do—for skills, for judgment, for experience, for education, for intelligent and mature attention to so much in so many places —world-wide—and that all of us are better off earnestly occupied. And the cut from activity to inactivity need not, perhaps, be so sharp, if men pursue their full powers to the best of their ability while yet they live in this life, and then move on to the great and limitless assurances and possibilities of everlasting life.

In the meaningful words of an eminent American: "Help us, O Lord, truly to live!"[165]

At Summer's End...

The passing of any season is somewhat sobering, or any day, or any period of the past. When a season begins, when a day begins, we think what we will do with it—what we haven't done—what we should do. At the beginning of summer, we think what we will do this summer season, with family, with friends, with many anticipated activities. But time runs us a race that it always wins, and seldom do we exceed—and much more frequently fail to do fully—what we felt we should have done, what we intended to do.

We are often torn between wanting to press much into life, and wanting to live in quiet content. No one can always continue in intense activity with full effectiveness, but anyone will deteriorate if he doesn't plan and continue in purposeful pursuit. Yet it little seems likely that on any day, or in any season, we will do everything we intended to do. There will always be work left undone. He who has done everything he intended to do, has lost his interest in life, or at least his best reason for living.

Creation is a continuing process, and we cannot conceive of a heaven or a hereafter, in which there will not be work to do, worlds to create and conquer. An eternity of idleness, of cloud-drifting inactivity, would be no heaven at all. Here or hereafter it is little likely that anyone would be content without the opportunity and incentive to be anxiously engaged in a good cause. Always we should set for ourselves a little more than we can accomplish, so that we will reach for it, but not become unduly discouraged because we don't fill the full measure of what we intended to do each day, or in any summer, or in any season—so long as earnestly we have something to show for the effort of the hours—something constructive to look to and say, "this I have done this day."

Thank God for the passing days, for the passing seasons, for the accomplishment of every hour, and for the one assuring fact that keeps us from an inconsolable frustration—the fact of the everlastingness of life, and that there will be work to do, and worlds to conquer, always and forever.

Autumn Leaves Its Lesson...

S omewhere we have read a sentence which says
"God is in the ... march of the seasons ..."[166]
At the season of harvest it seems to be so.

The changing of seasons is an always awesome sight. And awesome would it also be if one of them failed to follow in order. But blessedly the Creator and Administrator of heaven and earth has not left such things to chance: "He comprehendeth all things, and all things are before him, ... And ... he hath given a law unto all things, by which they move in their times and their seasons; ... and any man who hath seen any or the least of these hath seen God moving in his majesty and power."[167]

As to autumn, Lin Yutang gave us these sentences many seasons ago: ". . . I like spring," he said, "but it is too young. I like summer, but it is too proud. So I like best of all autumn, because its leaves are a little yellow, its tone mellower, its colors richer, and it is tinged a little with sorrow. . . . Its golden richness speaks not of the innocence of spring, nor of the power of summer, but of the mellowness and kindly wisdom of approaching age. It knows the limitations of life and is content."[168] Such are some thoughts on the mellowing mood of autumn—a season that leaves its lesson—the lesson that before the harvest there are the plowing, and the planting, the period of preparation. There are always cause and consequence, and the ever-present importance of improving, of repenting, and of performing the work that each season suggests.

"Cause and effect," said Emerson, "means and ends, seed and fruit, cannot be severed; for the effect already blooms in the cause, the end pre-exists in the means, the fruit in the seed. . . . There is a third silent party to all our bargains. The nature and soul of things takes on itself the guaranty of the fulfillment of every contract, so that honest service cannot come to loss. . . . Every stroke shall be repaid."[36]

And so it is—and so is the autumn season, with its law of harvest, of cause and consequence, of return for the plowing and the planting, for the preparation—and autumn suggests that youth should look to itself while yet there is time to prepare, for the "seed and fruit, cannot be severed."[36]

"Where One Door Shuts, Another Opens..."

There is maxim quoted in Don Quixote which says: "Where one door shuts, another opens. . . ."[169] We come to an end, and find a beginning.

Often we worry about arriving at an end, with too little faith in what follows. In any year, in any day, we are given to worrying about much that has happened, much that hasn't happened, much that doesn't happen. With problems, with disappointments, and sometimes in sorrow, the question comes to troubled hearts: "What am I going to do now?" The answer inevitably is, continue to do what needs to be done, what can be done; to do the necessary things, and have the faith to know that life will unfold, as it always has, as it continues to do. "Where one door shuts, another opens . . ."—and we have to have the faith to move through the open door and face the facts.

If we have obligations, we must do our best to meet them; if debts, we must do our best to pay them. If we have duties, we must do them. If we have limitations and impairments, we must learn to live with them, or rise above them.

And as to old errors, we must learn from them, and repent from the errors of the past—but not waste life in brooding or wishing we had done differently. The fact is we didn't do differently, and this is where we are, and this is where we must begin again—with a reaching out in reasonableness and righteousness, with a willingness to try, with a willingness to work, with a willingness to leave the past with as little regret as possible; to repent and improve, with gratitude, with courage, with conviction, with dignity, with faith, and with a resolve to face facts, and to improve upon the past. This is where we are—"Where one door shuts, another opens. . . ." We come to an end and find a beginning.

> "To fight the unbeatable foe
> And never to stop dreaming or fighting—
> This is man's privilege
> And the only life worth living."[170]

* * *

> "May peace be with you,
>   this day—and always."

Index of References to
Quoted Passages

29. Carlyle, *Inaugural Address,* 57
30. Charles F. Kettering, quoted in *Time,* Dec. 8, 1958, 60
31. Richardson Packe, 61
32. Book of Mormon, Alma 41:10, 66
33. Accredited to J. Edgar Hoover, 68
34. William James, 69
35. Shakespeare, *Hamlet,* Act i, 70
36. Emerson, *Compensation,* 72, 93, 167, 234
37. August W. Hare, 72
38. Sir James M. Barrie, 73
39. Carlyle, *Past and Present,* 76
40. Dr. Orlando A. Battista, *How to Enjoy Work and Get More Fun Out of Life,* 77
41. Schopenhauer, *Counsels and Maxims,* 77
42. Will Durant, *The Story of Philosophy,* Schopenhauer, ch. vii, 77
43. Voltaire, *In Sainte-Beuve,* i, 78, 226
44. Henri De Man, *Joy in Work,* 78
45. Irwin Edman, *On American Leisure,* 78, 83
46. Carl F. H. Henry, Ph.D., *The Dignity of Work, Vital Speeches,* Aug. 15, 1954, 80
47. Treglown, *The Christian and His Daily Work,* 80
48. Doctrine and Covenants 58:27, 80
49. New Testament: John 17:4, 81
50. Daniel Wolsey Vorhees, address delivered in the House of Representatives, March 9, 1864, 81
51. John Ruskin, *Work,* Lecture I, 82
52. Maurice Linden, M.C., *The Human Life Cycle,* 83
53. Cicero, *On Old Age,* 84, 225, 226, 228, 229, 230
54. William Penn, The Preface: *The Fruits of Solitude,* 87
55. J. A. Hatfield, 87
56. Old Testament: Proverbs 23:7, 87, 92
57. Michelangelo, 88
58. Emerson, *The American Scholar,* 88
59. Thomas à Kempis, *Imitation of Christ,* 89
60. New Testament: I Thessalonians 5:22, 92
61. Doctrine and Covenants 130:20, 21, 93, 94, 128
62. *Pascal's Thoughts,* 99, 100
63. Gustaf Stromberg, *The Soul of the Universe,* 99
64. Chinese Proverb, 100
65. William Feather, 101
66. Arthur P. Stanley, *Our Common Christianity,* 102
67. William Penn, *More Fruits of Solitude,* 102
68. Quoted by Montaigne, *Of Solitude,* accredited to Horace, 103, 141, 142

[238]

69. *Ibid.*, accredited to Socrates, 103
70. Emerson, *Self-Reliance,* 103
71. Montaigne, *Of Solitude,* 104
72. Caleb C. Colton, 104, 207
73. Emerson, 104, 122
74. William Paley, 105
75. Accredited to Carlyle, 107
76. Accredited to Emerson, 109
77. An approximate quotation accredited to Dr. Samuel Johnson, 109
78. Air Commodore W. C. Cooper, *Character and Its Place in Industry,* Rotary, R.I.B.I. Vol. 2, No. 24, 111, 115, 122
79. Joseph L. Townsend, 112
80. George Washington, 113
81. Alexander Pope, *Essay on Man,* 113
82. Herbert Spencer, 113, 122
83. *George Washington,* by Douglas Southall Freeman, 113
84. Anne Morrow Lindbergh, *Gift from the Sea,* 116
85. Old Testament: Psalm 32:2, 121
86. Marcus Aurelius Antoninus, 121
87. Arthur P. Stanley, 122
88. Edmund Burke, 123
89. Katharine Lee Bates, *America, the Beautiful,* 125
90. Cecil B. DeMille, Brigham Young University Commencement Address, 1957, 126
91. Doctrine and Covenants 88:34, 128
92. William E. Gladstone, *Kin Beyond Sea,* 131
93. Joseph Smith, *The Principle of Religion,* 131
94. Doctrine and Covenants 101:80, 131
95. Florence E. Allen, Commencement Address, University of Utah, 1960, 132
96. George Washington, *Farewell Address,* 132
97. Andrew Jackson, *Farewell Address,* 132, 134
98. Daniel Webster (quoted by Joseph Roswell Hawley in an address titled *On the Flag and the Eagle,* 1874), 133
99. Charles Kingsley, 134
100. Robert G. Ingersoll, *The Christian Religion,* 135
101. Doctrine and Covenants 88:118, 138
102. Edwin Hubbell Chapin, *Eulogy of Horace Greeley,* 139
103. Charles Reade, 140
104. Phillips Brooks, *Sermons: Purpose and Use of Comfort,* 140
105. Samuel Johnson, 140
106. Richardson Packe, 144

107. Jean-Antoine Petit-Senn, 149
108. Shakespeare, *Henry VIII*, Act iii, 149
109. Austin Phelps, 149
110. Joseph Addison, 149
111. Sir Walter Raleigh, *To the History of the World*, 149
112. New Testament: Hebrews 13:18, 149
113. New Testament: Philippians 4:8, 149
114. Jean Jacques Rousseau, *A Savoyard Vicar*, 150
115. Henri Bergson, *Criticism*, 151
116. Matthew Cowley, *Matthew Cowley Speaks*, 154
117. Donald Grant Mitchell, *Reveries of a Bachelor*, 161, 198
118. Justice Oliver Wendell Holmes, cited in *Yankee from Olympus*, 161
119. Emerson, *Spiritual Laws*, 163
120. *Ibid.*, *The Over-Soul*, 164
121. John C. Lavater, 165
122. Bruce Barton, *If a Man Dies, Shall He Live Again?* 167
123. Book of Mormon, Alma 34:38, 168
124. *Ibid.*, Mosiah 2:20-22, 168
125. New Testament: Hebrews 11:1, 169
126. Doctrine and Covenants 59:21, 170
127. Shakespeare, *Henry VI*, 172
128. Old Testament: Joshua 24:2-14, 173
129. Shakespeare, *As You Like It*, Act ii, 177
130. Old Testament: Malachi 4:6, 178
131. Friedrich Nietzsche, cited by Will Durant, *The Story of Philosophy*, 178
132. Seneca, 179
133. Sir Richard Livingstone, quoted by Robert Redfield in *Creation and Education*, 181
134. Accredited to Thomas A. Edison in *There Is No Unanswered Prayer*, by Margaret Blair Johnstone, 192
135. Owen Feltham, 192
136. Edward G. Bulwer-Lytton, 193
137. New Testament: Matthew 18:16, 195
138. Doctrine and Covenants 76:22, 196
139. Old Testament: Job 19:25, 196
140. New Testament: John 3:16, 197
141. Old Testament: Genesis 1:25, 199
142. George Macdonald, *Songs of Spring Days*, 201
143. Tennyson, *Early Spring*, 201
144. Goethe, 201
145. New Testament: Acts 1;3,9-11, 202
146. *Plutarch's Lives*, 203
147. Jean Paul Richter, 205

148. James Bryce, Address to the Students of Rutgers, 1911, 210

149. Old Testament: Ecclesiastes 2:14, 211

150. Benjamin Franklin, *The Way to Wealth,* 211

151. Chesley R. Perry, 213

152. Old Testament: *see* Jeremiah 8:20, 215

153. *Quarterly Magazine,* Rotary International in Great Britain, Nov., 1959, 215

154. Thomas Hood, *Ode to Autumn,* 215

155. Accredited to Arthur Brisbane, 217

156. Arthur Brisbane, 220

157. Henry Wadsworth Longfellow, *Morituri Salutamus,* 221, 223, 224, 225

158. George Bernard Shaw, 228

159. Edward J. Stieglitz, *The Personal Challenge of Aging,* 228

160. Addison, *Cato,* Act iv, 228

161. John Ruskin, *Ad Valorem,* 228

162. Hadley, 228

163. Hugo Grotius, *Last Words,* 230

164. Carlyle, *Characteristics,* 230

165. David O. McKay, 230

166. John Lanahan, 233

167. Doctrine and Covenants 88:41, 42, 47, 233

168. Lin Yutang, *My Country and My People,* 233

169. Cervantes, maxim quoted in *Don Quixote,* 235

170. Dale Wasserman, *I, Don Quixote,* 236

Index of Subjects

[243]

[244]

[245]

[248]

[249]

[255]